50 Billion Dollar Boss

50 Billion Dollar Boss

African American Women Sharing Stories of Success in Entrepreneurship and Leadership

Kathey Porter and Andrea Hoffman

First published 2016 by
PALGRAVE MACMILLAN

The authors have asserted their rights to be identified as the authors of this work in accordance with the Copyright, Designs and Patents Act 1988.

Palgrave Macmillan in the UK is an imprint of Macmillan Publishers Limited, registered in England, company number 785998, of Houndmills, Basingstoke, Hampshire, RG21 6XS.

Palgrave Macmillan in the US is a division of Nature America, Inc., One New York Plaza, Suite 4500, New York, NY 10004-1562.

Palgrave Macmillan is the global academic imprint of the above companies and has companies and representatives throughout the world.

Hardback ISBN: 978–1–137–47501–5
E-PUB ISBN: 978–1–137–47503–9
E-PDF ISBN: 978–1–137–47502–2
DOI: 10.1057/9781137475022

Distribution in the UK, Europe and the rest of the world is by Palgrave Macmillan®, a division of Macmillan Publishers Limited, registered in England, company number 785998, of Houndmills, Basingstoke, Hampshire RG21 6XS.

Library of Congress Cataloging-in-Publication Data

Porter, Kathey.
    50 billion dollar boss : African American women sharing stories of success in entrepreneurship and leadership / Kathey Porter, Andrea Hoffman.
        pages cm
    Summary: "This book looks at several successful African American women and chronicles their success, obstacles, challenges, and lessons learned. The authors have first person access to each of these women and break down their stories to help other aspiring entrepreneurs achieve their dreams of starting or owning their own business"—Provided by publisher.
    Includes bibliographical references and index.
    ISBN 978–1–137–47501–5 (hardback)
        1. African American women—United States. 2. Women-owned business enterprises—United States. 3. Leadership in women—United States. I. Hoffman, Andrea, 1965– II. Title. III. Title: Fifty billion dollar boss.
HQ1438.U5P67 2015
305.48'896073—dc23   2015016499

A catalogue record of the book is available from the British Library.

Contents

Contents

Preface: Our Personal Journeys to Entrepreneurship and the Book

Kathey

For as long as I can remember, I have always wanted to be a business-woman. I've always had what people call a hustle. Even in elementary school, I would wear suits for picture day. In college, I always knew I wanted to major in business. I'm not sure whether this desire was the result of working with my mother making and selling jelly or selling dinners at the church, or me hawking Girl Scout cookies, but I always knew that I was going to do something in business. I just was not sure what I wanted to do in business.

My first introduction to a potential career in business occurred in high school. I saw the movie *Trading Places* with Eddie Murphy and Dan Ackroyd, where Ackroyd played a wealthy commodities broker and Murphy was the street-savvy hustler. Murphy and Ackroyd "traded places," with each assuming the other's life. Murphy quickly deduced that brokers were just educated bookies, and easily adapted to and succeeded in his new role. It was at this moment that I decided that I wanted to be a commodities broker, not because I knew exactly what they did, but because they made a lot of money doing it. I set out to learn everything I could about becoming a commodities broker.

After graduating from high school, I went to Mercer University in Macon, Georgia. I decided I would major in economics, and registered for my first class—microeconomics. Unfortunately, at 18, I did not understand the concept of supply and demand, and deservedly received an F. I went on to fail this class two more times in addition to flunking out my first year of college. I learned two things. First, in college you need to actually *go to class*, and second, being a commodities broker was probably not in the stars for me.

With lots of time on my hands and living near an army base, I decided to join the National Guard. While it was not a career choice, it turned into a life-changing experience. Because of my college experience, I entered the Guard at a higher rank than many of the other soldiers in my company. While in basic training, I was selected for various leadership roles and received a commendation as an expert M-16 weapons firer.

When I completed basic training and returned home, I did so with part-time employment and monthly VA payments to use for enrolling as a full-time student. After my disastrous first year at Mercer, I was now responsible for paying my own way through school. I transferred to Savannah State University (SSU) where my older sister was. We got an apartment together, and thus began my life at SSU. Unlike before, I went to every class and joined every study group available to ensure that I did not fail another class ever again.

Through the student loan repayment program, I graduated from college debt free, and bought my first house when I was 26. It was not until years later that I realized this experience had provided me with my first opportunity to really explore and experience leadership capabilities and aspirations that I never knew that I had. Ultimately, I stayed in the National Guard for six years.

With my college degree in hand, I had no idea what I wanted to do. I got a job as a sales assistant at a company called Carson

Products Company. At the time, while I was very familiar with the brands, I was not familiar with the company, and had no idea that their products were manufactured in Savannah, Georgia. Carson Products Company was a multimillion-dollar company that manufactured products for multicultural consumers, specifically African American consumers. The most popular products were the Dark & Lovely brand of relaxers, hair color, and haircare products, and Magic Shave (years later, the company was acquired by L'Oreal). Within a year, I moved to the marketing department as a brand assistant. I was quickly promoted and became an assistant brand manager, which allowed me to work on a smaller brand.

After about two years, I found out I was expecting my first child, my daughter, Hollis. When I returned to work, after about a year, I was named brand manager for the new line of products called Compositions. This was a product line for professional stylists, and gave me an opportunity to learn the professional salon industry. I was ecstatic, and this was an exciting time. However, I learned how fleeting this feeling can be and how vulnerable I was.

After about 18 months, the company decided the line was not growing at a rate fast enough for them, and they discontinued it! Although I was disappointed, I was promoted to brand manager for Dark & Lovely, the crown jewel of the company. Wow! This achievement was beyond any expectation that I had had when I had started with the company four years earlier. Being responsible for a multimillion-dollar brand and the flagship brand for the company was amazing, but it brought a new level of visibility, accountability, and scrutiny. The job was demanding, the hours long, and the travel exhausting. I began to feel like I was putting in a lot of hours for someone else's business. I came to learn that the term for what I was feeling was "burned out."

Additionally, I began to realize that, for the amount of time required to perform the job, I wanted more say and control over the entire operation of an entity, not just one aspect of it. Also, as a new mother, the quality of my time with my daughter was greatly diminished because I was working so many hours.

Increasingly, I became convinced that I had achieved everything that I could at the company. I left Carson and went back to school full time to pursue my MBA. Upon graduating, I accepted a position as group multicultural manager (marketing director) at Revlon Professional/Colomer USA in New York City. While I was glad to be working and loved the city, I began to resent the long hours and became wracked with guilt over missing my daughter's "firsts," school events (I didn't even know her teacher's name), and other important milestones. I needed a change.

As I thought about what I wanted to do and was passionate about, I realized the previous eight years had been such a whirlwind—successfully crafting a career as a marketing executive, having a child, buying a house, obtaining my MBA—that I never had time to give this any deliberate consideration. I always thought I was doing what I wanted to do. Despite my success and accomplishments, I was, yet again, at a crossroads in my career. Increasingly, I realized I wanted to pursue opportunities that allowed me more control and input in developing and implementing a company's overall strategic vision. However, financially, I was not ready to give up the security and standard of living that I had been able to provide for my family. Additionally, as my daughter was getting older, for the first time in my career, my work/life balance was becoming increasingly important. Now that I really considered what I wanted to do, I knew that, while I was probably too young and inexperienced to become the CEO of a big company, I wasn't too young to become the CEO of my own company. Once I had pondered and prayed, I set out to make this new vision a reality.

I took some start-up money from my retirement and enlisted two former colleagues to help start our own haircare line. They would bring the sales and distribution expertise, and I would work on the product development and marketing. I started working with a manufacturer in Chicago on product samples and with a local graphic designer on packaging designs. I lined up meetings with potential investors from my days in New York. I began working on the marketing plan with the manufacturer and graphic designer.

While trying to close the investors, I noticed that my two partners were not nearly as responsive or available as I needed them to be in order to get a project like this off the ground. Initially I blew it off, thinking they were just busy, as each of them had full-time jobs and were participating in this venture on a part-time basis. Unlike them, this was my brainchild and my full-time focus. Increasingly, it would be weeks before we would speak, and when we did, it felt like nothing was really accomplished. After about six months and a small investment on my part, my partners backed out. This experience taught me a valuable lesson about selecting the right team and surrounding myself with like-minded people. Once my partners dropped out, the investor decided to back out as well, leaving me to consider whether to continue pursuing the project on my own. While I had faith in my ability to work in a company or in the security of a group, I did question my ability to pull off something like this by myself. Also, I did not have nearly the resources needed to succeed, nor did I think I could get investors without partners. I ultimately decided this was too massive an undertaking and this was probably not the time to pursue something like this on my own. This was the first of many times where I questioned my confidence.

Then panic began to set in. If I'm not doing this, *then what am I going to do?*

I needed to own my own business.

I had some experience at this. My first business had been a consulting company, KP Group Marketing, which I had started during my final year in graduate school. My niche was in providing support to small businesses. I had clients ranging from Internet start-ups to hair salons and barbershops. I had also picked up work as a subcontractor to friends with larger firms doing promotions for Coca-Cola and L'Oreal. One of the largest projects that I worked on was with a minority construction firm that had just been awarded a $50 million construction project. However, while I was happy consulting, I was not bringing in enough money to support my family.

My next venture came about accidentally. I was considering several opportunities and came across an ad looking for store managers or owners for a seasonal store in the mall. The company was Calendar Club, a division of Barnes & Noble and a franchiser of calendar and game kiosks in malls across the United States and Canada. I had retail experience and had worked in the mall all through college, so I was familiar with the rigors of working during the holiday season. I thought that if nothing else, this would give me a great opportunity to determine whether retail was the entrepreneurial path that I wanted to pursue in the long run.

After weeks of vetting, I decided I had nothing to lose and applied for the franchise as an owner in the Savannah market. My application was approved and I enlisted a partner, which, soon after the store opened, I realized was an unnecessary mistake. Once again, I allowed my lack of confidence to limit my ability to pursue my dream and maximize my earning potential. Despite the arrangement, overnight, I was again an entrepreneur. I was the only African American and the only woman with a business in the mall. I was nervous and excited at the same time. The business model was a total turnkey operation. The parent company leased equipment (fixtures, cash register, software, and inventory) to franchisees, and the franchisees were responsible for personnel salaries, taxes, and all fees associated with the business, including telephone service, licenses, and permits. In return, the company took a percentage of profits each week. Inventory was replenished weekly based on sales, and at the end of the season during reconciliation, franchisees received a credit for all unsold merchandise. Having worked in the mall before, I knew the mall managers and was able to select the prime placement in the mall. While the franchise model was designed to be a kiosk, management allowed me to have an inline store using a space that was not being leased to another tenant. I got off to a slow start, but as I settled in, business began to pick up. The company headquarters distributed a weekly newsletter with updates for the stores across the country, the names of the top-performing stores, and general information to increase sales. Imagine my surprise when for one week during the busy holiday season, we were named one of the top ten stores in the United States and Canada.

Opening the store was one of the hardest things that I had ever done, yet one of the most rewarding and exhilarating. For the next two holiday seasons, the business was a family affair, with my sister and my daughter and her friends coming to work on the weekends, running the register and assisting customers. By the third season, based on my success during the two previous seasons, the company offered me two additional stores in another market. These were larger stores that also included games. However, while I had been confident and successful with one store, I was not sure about three. After much consideration, though, I finally accepted. Despite the hard work, long hours involved, and uncertainty after the season ended, I realized I was happiest when I was running the store. My team now consisted of ten employees, including a store manager and a staff of nine part-time employees.

After three years of the business and working during the holidays (rather than enjoying them), I finally decided I had had enough. I wanted an opportunity that would allow me to use my background in marketing and product development. I started looking at products in stores and categories where I thought I might have the most success creating a product for a multicultural consumer. I finally decided on the home category and created a multicultural children's bedding line called KidFlava. I found an artist to create designs and found a manufacturer in China with the hopes of getting distribution in national retail stores. Because there were few products targeting this consumer, I thought this would be an easy proposition. I later found out that this is one of the toughest categories to enter and that getting a product on the shelves is a time-consuming and costly investment. Fortunately, this was right around the time when online stores were becoming increasingly popular, providing an opportunity for small start-ups like mine to sell their products directly to consumers.

I recently launched BusinessFAB Enterprises, a multimedia company that recognizes, supports, and connects fearless, awesome, boss (FAB) women to business opportunities. We conduct entrepreneurship workshops and networking events for women in business who are looking to create opportunities, connect with other women in business, and cultivate success in business and in life. I recently formed a partnership with a government agency to conduct entrepreneurship workshops for start-ups and emerging entrepreneurs.

In 2009, I started researching and reading about women entrepreneurs. While I did not set out to write a book, I began to see the impact that African American women were having on our economy and the rate at which they were starting businesses. I starting thinking about the women whom I knew and met across the country, yet very little was ever written about them. The project morphed into this book, showcasing these women, their successes, and their advice on how to get through tough times when starting, building, and maintaining a business.

As an adjunct instructor, I receive tons of textbooks and books each year. I received Andrea's book, *Black is the New Green: Marketing to Affluent African Americans*, and immediately became a fan. Based on her background, her extensive knowledge of the multicultural market, and the expertise of her firm, I thought she might be an interesting person to partner with. Several years later we were introduced. When I told her about my idea, she immediately got it!

We are very proud and excited share our book with you.

Andrea

In 2006, I launched Diversity Affluence. My effort was driven by a single mission: to paint a more accurate picture of the size, scope, and social and economic clout of affluent African Americans, part of a group I refer to as *royaltons*. I coined this term in 2006 to define affluent multicultural (nonwhite) consumers.

My desire to embark on this mission was sparked around 2001 when I was working as an agency executive on a Mercedes Benz account. I was a marketing communications strategist honing my expertise in target marketing and business development for luxury brands. During a meeting with thought leaders from Yanelovick (now called The Futures Company), who were presenting my team and the Mercedes client with demographic insight to help inform our new product launch and marketing efforts, something came over me: insight on emerging markets. I'm not sure that anyone else in the room spotted this important (growing or lasting) demographic shift, but I did. It was as if my calling had found me.

For me, it was like there was a thousand-pound neon-green elephant in the room.

Since then, my commitment has played out in groundbreaking research reports and resources guides, bespoke events connecting upscale brands to affluent African Americans, invite-only convenings with African American influencers, business strategy consulting, and the coauthoring of the book *Black is the New Green: Marketing to Affluent African Americans*. When I published my book in 2010, I recall incorporating an idea that I fully expected marketers to acknowledge and embrace: that Black women were an audience to engage.

Fast-forward three years later. I received a call from a friend who wanted to introduce me to Kathey Porter. She had an idea for a book and wanted me to coauthor it. She presented her idea and then patiently waited for my schedule to free up, and *50 Billion Dollar Boss* was born!

As a serial entrepreneur myself, starting at the age of 18, I'm proud to be a part of this body of work. I'm equally proud to provide a platform online and offline, for knowledge and wisdom so that other women entrepreneurs can feel less alone and more informed in order to fully realize their passion, purpose, and potential.

I read a quote recently that rings true for me, and I'm sure it will for you too: "Entrepreneurs sacrifice security for opportunity." My biggest wish for you as a reader and businesswoman is that you forge forward with your eyes wide open and never quit when times get tough. Remember that your spirit knows things before your brain does, so always, always, always trust your instinct. It may not be able to speak out loud, but it will certainly speak volumes if you pay attention.

Acknowledgments

Kathey

I started this project in 2009, and have worked on it off and on since then. At the time, I was not really sure what it was going to be, but, without a doubt, the final product is beyond my expectations. It was worth the wait to find the right team to bring this project to light. I hope that, in addition to being inspired by the stories included in the book, you are guided in knowing that if you have a dream or an idea that you think is wild, crazy, or beyond anything that you are doing now, stick with it! It only takes one yes to totally change the trajectory of a project.

First, I would like to thank my coauthor, Andrea—the right partner, at the right time, for the right project. Andrea's informal mentorship and guidance through this project and in business has been invaluable. I would also like to thank our editor, Laurie Harting, who believed in this project and fully embraced it from the start. I appreciate her patience, thoughtfulness, honesty, and gentle nudging to make this project the best that it could be.

Thank you to my family, my daughter, Hollis, and my ten-year old son, Mason, who did not hesitate to tell me when I needed to "work on it a little more." I want to thank my informal editorial crew who read and reread without hesitation and constantly called, texted, and e-mailed to check up on me to ensure that I was getting this done. I want to especially thank Dr. Wanda Smith, Associate Professor of Management in the Pamplin College of Business at Virginia Tech, my biggest cheerleader, advisor, mentor, and friend, who started every conversation with "how's the book coming?" and always pushed me to stay motivated and focused on the reader. You were right... this moment feels AMAZING!

Thanks to all of the women business owners whom I have met, counseled, trained, and learned from over the years. Your enthusiasm, drive, and passion excite and inspire me, and I hope you enjoy this book as much as I have enjoyed bringing it to you.

Finally, I want to thank the ladies in this book who graciously agreed to participate in this project, willingly and enthusiastically sharing their stories and experiences. This experience was as enriching and enlightening as it was fun. I am truly a fan!

Andrea

I'd like to thank our editor, Laurie Harting, for her openness to new ideas and willingness to, specifically, embrace *50 Billion Dollar Boss*. I value our relationship and learn something new from her with each interaction. I would also like to thank my coauthor, Kathey Porter, whose idea it was to write this book. Kathey inspires me with her fearless pursuit of her dreams and generous spirit.

This book could not have been completed without the love, support, and encouragement of my best female friends (Vicky, Michon, D'Metriss), who believe in me and love me, warts and all. They fill my emotional, spiritual, and intellectual gas tank when it's empty and turn into comedians when I'm in desperate need of nature's best medicine, laughing out loud. And of course, a heart felt thank you to my mother, Wilma, whom I affectionately refer to as (B.O.W.) (an inside joke), one of the nicest people I've ever known. A woman who has dedicated her life to learning something new each and every day. A woman who taught me from an early age to give back and pay it forward.

Lastly, I'd like to share some wisdom I've learned along the way in hopes that you continue forging meaningful bonds with other grounded women. "As individual women, our ideas and passions may in fact be exciting and profound, but it's together with other women who support and believe in us, no matter what, that we can be truly transformative in our vision and accomplishments during our short time on this earth."

Introduction: A New Boss in Town

"Why hasn't this been done before?"

That was one of the questions we asked when starting this project. The more we thought about it, the more our motivation and enthusiasm for this book grew within us. We wanted to create something that both highlighted the accomplishments of the women profiled and was something that we wish we had been able to reference when starting our own businesses. Although our paths to entrepreneurship have been very different, we share a mutual interest in the success of women-owned businesses. Further, as practitioners of diversity, we frequently meet and come into contact with dynamic African American women who are starting or running amazing businesses. Unfortunately, many aspiring entrepreneurs are not familiar with these leaders, achievers, and pioneers. For too long there have been few "roadmaps" for young women entrepreneurs—particularly African American women entrepreneurs—to follow. While women are starting businesses in unprecedented numbers, many African Americans are first-generation entrepreneurs, and there have been few role models for them to emulate and learn from. Resources and opportunities to establish these crucial relationships have been lacking.

The impact of African American women in business is undeniable. According to *The 2014 State of Women-Owned Businesses Report* commissioned by American Express OPEN, while firms owned by women of color are smaller than nonminority women-owned businesses, their growth in both numbers and economic clout is generally far outpacing that of other women-owned entities. Businesses owned by African American women led that growth, up 296 percent from 1997 to 2014, and generated nearly $50 billion in revenue.

Fifty billion dollars is a surprisingly big number—and hence the title of this book.

Whether women entrepreneurs are thinking about starting a business or looking to take an existing business to new heights, this book is a guide to help them clarify their vision, build relationships, find resources, sustain the business, and identify growth opportunities for the future. Each of the women featured in this book has built a successful business and is respected, revered, and looked upon as a thought leader in her respective industry. Many of the women profiled have self-funded their ventures. All learned many poignant lessons along the way, which they graciously share. Despite the societal label of being a "double minority," they have been able to use their passion and skills to do what African American women always do: make money, provide for their families, and uplift their communities.

African American women continue to excel and shape society across industries. This book recognizes them for their business acumen and examines how they creatively solve business challenges and identify opportunities to grow and sustain their businesses.

These women are *rock stars*!

CHAPTER 1

The Growing Impact of African American Women-Owned Businesses

When you think about the black community, entrepreneurship has always been a huge part of our heritage. It was inevitable that black women would become a force in the business community. We all have mommas, aunties, and "Big Mommas," who, for years, have cooked, "did" hair, or kept kids on the side. When you look at black entrepreneurship today, communities across the country from the North to the South are jam-packed with these same types of businesses. Black women have long been community leaders and are now moving from being the emotional backbone of the country to becoming a greater economic force. By starting their own companies, African American women are reinvesting money back into the community by creating jobs, providing much-needed services and products, and serving as role models of business success.

It is, in a sense, a second Black Renaissance. We have all heard stories of how, in the late nineteenth and the early twentieth century, the black community was robust and healthy, with examples of black entrepreneurship and enterprise at every conceivable level. For example, the scholarly work of Dr. Juliet E. K. Walker, author of *The History of Black Business in America* (among many other works), shows that even since the days of slavery, entrepreneurship has always run strong among black Americans. Black businessmen and businesswomen thrived even before the Civil War, creating a class of entrepreneurs and creative capitalists.

Perhaps the most widely known early African American woman entrepreneur was Madame C. J. Walker, who in 1907 created a line of haircare products targeting African American consumers. It was her hiring in 1905 by Annie Turnbo-Malone, another haircare entrepreneur who is widely recognized for her role in launching the

African American haircare industry, which set the stage for African American women to succeed as entrepreneurs. By 1920, Turnbo-Malone's net worth was reportedly $14 million, a phenomenal feat by today's standards, let alone in 1920. Not only were Walker and Turnbo-Malone successful entrepreneurs but they both used their wealth and success to uplift the black community. Both women overcame what could only be described as insurmountable obstacles to become outstanding entrepreneurs, philanthropists, community catalysts, and lasting examples of what we as African American women can accomplish despite the odds.

Unfortunately, in the twentieth century the promise of black emancipation and full rights of citizenship were countered by powerful negative forces; consequently, as research shows, the rate of black entrepreneurship *declined* steadily throughout the century. Reasons include increased racial hostility from the established wealthy classes, competition from immigrant groups, and difficulties originating from the lack of public policies.

Ironically, the decline of black entrepreneurship has been linked to integration. Many experts suggest that before integration, black-owned businesses flourished because blacks were unwelcome in white-owned businesses. Blacks built businesses that were patronized by other blacks simply because they had no choice. Integration threw *open* the doors to competition, but institutionalized racism kept *closed* the doors to education and finance. Forced to compete on a playing field that was not level, black businesses closed, one by one.

Most cities across America have a Martin Luther King Jr. Street, Boulevard, or Drive, or an equivalent, which in its heyday served as the hub of economic activity for the African American community. Over the years, with integration, assimilation, and greater economic access, black businesses evolved dramatically, resulting in what can only be described as the ironic decimation of these hubs as the centers of black entrepreneurship. In this new century, the good news is that African American entrepreneurship is once again on the rise. It has adapted and positioned itself to achieve unimaginable heights that span the spectrum of industries and disciplines.

Any discussion of modern-day entrepreneurship by African American women would not be complete without including Oprah Winfrey, who by anyone's scale is one of the most successful entrepreneurs of our time. But she is not alone. It is not uncommon to see famous faces such as Tyra Banks and Iman who have become entrepreneurs.

According to the 2014 State of Women-Owned Businesses Report commissioned by American Express OPEN, since 1997 the number of African American women-owned firms has grown by 296 percent, leading all ethnic categories of women-owned businesses. Armed with corporate experience (and some with MBAs, JDs, or PhDs), whether just starting a career or launching a second career, African American women have entered the business arena ready to do both battle and business with their male counterparts and even with the corporate giants where they once worked. These adventurers are carving out new territory in the marketplace, providing an array of products and services, and building exciting, successful enterprises in highly competitive industries including cosmetics, fashion, hospitality, food, construction, and many more.

The report further states that in 1997 there were just under one million (929,445) firms owned by women of color, accounting for one in six, or 17 percent, of women-owned firms. As of 2014, that number had skyrocketed to an estimated 2,934,500, and comprised one in three, or 32 percent, of women-owned firms. Further, when looking at the growth in the number, employment, and revenues of women-owned firms during the same period, growth rates among firms owned by women of color (albeit from a smaller base) are outshining growth rates among all women-owned firms. Within those 2.9 million firms owned by women of color, it is estimated that 1,237,900 were owned by African American women; 1,033,100 were

Latina-owned firms; 675,900 were Asian American women-owned firms; 119,900 firms were owned by Native American or Alaska Native women, and 20,000 were Native American/Pacific Islander women-owned firms.

While firms owned by women of color are smaller than nonminority women-owned businesses, both in terms of average employment and revenues, their growth in number and economic clout is generally far outpacing that of all women-owned firms. Indeed, from 1997 to 2014 the growth in the number of African American (+296%), Asian American (+179%), Latina (+206%), Native American/Alaska Native (124%), and Native Hawaiian/Pacific Islander (+247%) women-owned firms all top the growth in the number of nonminority women-owned firms (+32%).

Growth in employment (except among Native American/Alaska Native women-owned firms) and revenue growth are also stronger among firms owned by women of color than among nonminority women-owned firms. While this is due, in part, to growth from a smaller base number, it does indicate that business ownership is an ever more commonplace pursuit among women of color. Across the country, over two-thirds (69%) of minority-owned firms are found in ten states: California, Florida, Georgia, Illinois, Maryland, New Jersey, New York, North Carolina, Texas, and Virginia. And while nationally 29 percent of all firms and 32 percent of women-owned firms are owned by persons of color, in several of these states (California, Maryland, New York, and Texas), more than four in ten firms are owned by persons of color. Indeed, in 2014, just over half (52%) of businesses in New York were estimated to be minority owned.

Moving on Up...African American Women-Owned Firms

During 2014, firms owned by African American women numbered an estimated 1,237,900. These firms employed 287,100 workers and generated an estimated $49.5 billion in revenue. Overall, there are an estimated 2.5 million African American–owned firms in the United States, employing just over one million (1,013,700) workers and generating $170.9 billion in revenues. African American women own fully 49 percent of all African American–owned firms, employ 28 percent of the workers employed by African American–owned firms, and contribute 29 percent of the revenue generated by African American–owned businesses. Since 1997, the number of African American women-owned firms has grown by 296 percent, employment has risen 70 percent, and revenues have climbed 265 percent—in comparison with 68 percent firm growth among all women-owned firms, 11 percent employment growth among all women-owned firms, and 72 percent revenue growth among all women-owned firms.

Nearly two-thirds (61%) of African American women-owned firms are found in ten states. The greatest numbers of African American women-owned firms are located in New York (126,800), followed by Georgia (108,900) and Texas (98,800). While African American women comprise 14 percent of all women-owned firms nationally, African American women comprise the greatest share of all women-owned firms in Georgia (34%), Maryland (32%), and Illinois (22%). As previously stated, the number of African American women-owned firms nationally has climbed 296 percent since 1997, while employment is up 70 percent and revenues have risen by 265 percent.

Among the ten most populous states for minority-owned firms, the states seeing the fastest growth in the number of African American women owned firms are Georgia (up 430%), Texas (up 376%), and Illinois (up 320%). In North Carolina, while the number of African American women-owned firms has increased by 267 percent since 1997, employment has risen by 361 percent and revenues are up 408 percent, making African American women-owned firms in the Tar Heel State among the most economically robust in the United States.

Why Women of Color Are Becoming Business Owners at Increasing Rates

In a recent policy brief, Farah Z. Ahmad (2014), policy analyst for Progress 2050 at the Center for American Progress, explored the undeniable impact women of color are having on the growth in entrepreneurship in the United States. Ahmad's brief explains possible contributing factors toward their interest in entrepreneurial pursuits, the unique challenges that they face, and what can be done to support and sustain their growth. "Some of the barriers that women of color face include limited access to mentors, exclusion from elite networks, and the gender wage gap," says Ahmad. But despite, or perhaps *because of,* the unique challenges women of color face in today's traditional workplace, their entrepreneurial spirit and impact are undeniable. Understanding women's roles and challenges in entrepreneurship—as well as the traditional workplace— is essential to ensure that women of color can succeed, lift themselves to greater heights, and help our economy thrive.

Whether it is challenges to workplace advancement, unequal pay, or a lack of social capital in a business world still dominated by white males, women of color have many reasons to become their own bosses. In fact, a Cox BLUE survey of women entrepreneurs found that 61 percent of women cited the opportunity to be their own boss as a reason to become an entrepreneur. Other top reasons included having greater control of their own destinies, desiring to pursue their passions, making more money than they could while working for someone else, and spending more time with their families and children.

Here are some of the top reasons.

Opportunity to be their own boss. Do *what* you want, *when* you want, *how* you want! This is a simplistic view, and in reality, there is always someone to answer to, including your customers and your investors. However, you do have greater control over all these, but only if you commit early on to a work/life balance.

Greater control of their own destinies. The days of job security are long gone. Many feel that the true path to any type of security, and thus controlling their fate, is through being their own boss and relying on their own instincts and outputs, and redefining what "success" is.

Desire to pursue their passions. Despite the myriad of accomplishments women have achieved, many women are reevaluating their purposes and are finding success and deeper fulfillment in creating businesses around their passions, whether it is volunteerism, working with nonprofits, pursuing crafts, or other engaging in causes that resonate with them.

Financial gain. Recently Catalyst, a group that does research and promotes business opportunities for women, examined Fortune 500 companies, and found that women hold only 17 percent of the seats on boards of directors. They have an even smaller share (about 15%) of senior executive positions. Despite all the talk about the value of increasing gender diversity at the top, change is happening very slowly. This lack of ability to reach the top echelons within existing corporate structures has many women rethinking whether it is worth it.

Desire for work/life balance. As women grow and progress in their careers, get married, and have families, priorities tend to shift, thus increasing the desire for greater work/life balance. While many women do not want to totally relinquish their outside, professional interests, they would like to balance this with the ability to have an active role in the lives of their families.

Flexibility to spend more time with family and children. Relevant, but not exclusive to African American women, is the fact that more than half will likely be unmarried and raising children in a single-family home. As more African American women are tasked with being the heads of household, their intent to provide a nurturing and stable environment does not wane. It is this intent that helps fuel their desire to have more control over their futures, have the flexibility to be active, involved, and engaged parents, and secure a financial future for themselves and their families.

CHAPTER 2

You Want to Do *What?* Turning Your Idea into Your Business

Dr. Lisa Williams, Founder, President and CEO World of EPI™, LLC and Creator of Positively Perfect™

Ask any entrepreneur and they will attest that business ideas are delivered in many forms. After years of working, some people see an opportunity and need in the marketplace and set out to fulfill the need. Some people say their idea came to them in a dream. Wherever the idea generates, once the decision is made to make the dream a reality, it is sometimes very difficult to share this vision, especially with people who do not share your same enthusiasm, excitement, and entrepreneurial tendencies, and are unable to provide the support, whether emotional or financial, needed to make your ideas and vision a reality.

Dr. Lisa Williams is internationally recognized as an academic trailblazer and an award-winning speaker and author. In 2003, she founded the multimillion-dollar company World of EPI™, LLC (Entertainment, Publishing and Inspiration). Walmart, EPI's largest customer, awarded her the 2013 Supplier of the Year Award for her visionary leadership. Working in partnership with several of the world's largest retailers, World of EPI™ reaches and touches the lives of an entire generation of children through its Positively Perfect™ Doll Line.

Dr. Lisa (as she is known) was also named an EY Entrepreneurial Winning Women Class (EWW) of 2013. EWW is a highly prestigious, nationally competitive award for which Ernst & Young, the global leader in accounting and financial services, handpicks some of the most promising women entrepreneurs. While her journey has been called a Cinderella story, she shares her story of how she was able to turn an idea into a multimillion dollar business.

A Storied Career

Becoming a successful, award-winning entrepreneur was not necessarily a part of Dr. Lisa's plan. She had what could be described as an incredible career in academia, marked with many firsts, including being the first African American female professor to earn tenure at Pennsylvania State University's Smeal College of Business, the first African American to receive a doctorate in Logistics from Ohio State University, and the first female professor to receive a multimillion dollar endowed chair in her field. She has won numerous teaching awards, including Outstanding Faculty Member of the Year from Penn State. She was designated as an "Amazing Woman" by the University of Nevada Las Vegas (UNLV), and received the Trailblazer Award from the American Marketing Association PhD Project. She has also received recognitions from major universities such as Penn State, Ohio State, and the University of Arkansas.

Known for her ability to motivate executives and future leaders, she has been featured in many magazines, and her expertise has been sought by major corporations and former president Bill Clinton's Commission on Critical Infrastructure Protection. Dr. Lisa has been ranked by the most prestigious journal in the field for the number of articles published. Her research has been published in the *Journal of Marketing Channels, Journal of Business Logistics, The Transportation Journal, The International Journal of Physical Distribution and Logistics Management*, and *The International Journal of Logistics Management*. Her column "Profiles in Leadership" has been published in *Supply Chain Management Review Magazine*.

Dr. Lisa's research has had practical and global implications, allowing her to travel the world and speak to audiences throughout the United States, Belgium, Austria, Canada, England, and Australia. Through hard work and perseverance, Dr. Lisa attained unprecedented success.

Then, at the height of her career, Dr. Lisa did the unthinkable... she left the academic life to blaze a new trail as an entrepreneur.

A Higher Calling

With numerous accolades and honors under her wings, Dr. Lisa had created and achieved a laudable path to success. But while on her journey of enlightening people through education, she realized that God required more of her. "I have several degrees and lots of education," she says, "and for a long time I leaned on that. When God brought this to me, yes, it required expertise, but it also required other traits that I had to develop. It required me to have a meditation and prayer life." Dr. Lisa had to tap into God's infinite knowledge and well of wisdom to see what He'd have her to do. She said she also learned to walk by faith and not by sight.

When she decided to start her company, people thought she was crazy, pointing out that she was a professor, not an entrepreneur. They asked her, "Why are you doing this?" But she viewed this as a higher calling, in which she could do more and give more. She was at a stage in her career when most people were looking to advance higher, but Dr. Lisa felt that she was compelled to follow her passion and do what God was telling her to do. "Sometimes following your heart and doing what God tells you doesn't always make sense," she says. Once she decided to follow her heart, though, all of those doubts and roadblocks gradually diminished. "When I would take a step, things and information would appear."

A Partnership Emerges

Because of her desire to improve literacy in the black community, Dr. Lisa started a publishing company called EPI Books. She published inspirational and children's books from several authors as well as books that she wrote. Her first book, *Leading Beyond Excellence*, which was a self-help/motivational book featuring several extremely successful military generals and CEOs, including H. Lee Scott, CEO of Walmart, did extremely well. She then published a series of children's stories incorporating all ethnicities—African American, Latina, Caucasian, and Asian.

At the time Dr. Lisa started publishing her books, she was a full professor in the Walton College of Business at the University of Arkansas. An internationally recognized researcher, she held a multimillion-dollar endowed chair, partially funded by Walmart and the Walton family. Unbeknowst to her at the time, the success of her books and characters caught the attention of Walmart executives. Her books showed Walmart she could offer something to the company's executives that they had been longing to do, which was to sell children's books that reflected multiculturalism. She believed she could tackle the job and was successful at helping to produce two additional books, *Brandon's Really Bad, Really Good Day* and *Amelia Asks Why?* Both books depicted African American children in a manner that young children of color could relate to.

After the success of publishing, Walmart requested a line of dolls based on the image and likeness of the characters in Dr. Lisa's successful children's series. The executives thought this strategy would further expand and solidify their footprint within the communities they served and believed a deeper partnership with Dr. Lisa was just the thing to do that.

Let Inspiration Find You

Wanting to stay in her comfort zone, which was publishing, Dr. Lisa was initially skeptical about creating a doll, and dismissed the idea because she knew nothing about doll manufacturing. In fact, Walmart approached her on numerous occasions about the idea, and Dr. Lisa turned them down each time.

Dr. Lisa believes that you should let inspiration find you. One day she was watching television and saw the Anderson Cooper special

Black and White: Kids on Race, which inspired her. She recalled seeing a beautiful little brown girl who thought her own skin was ugly and ashy. With a choice of dolls ranging from skin tones ranging from Caucasian to deep mocha, the little brown girl pointed to the white doll and said, "She's pretty."

"That was a sign to me," says Dr. Lisa. As she began to ponder the possibilities of a line of dolls, she began to recall her own experience as a youth. "There weren't any pretty African American dolls. All the pretty dolls were Caucasian. You can go through life thinking that Caucasians are the model of beauty, and that African Americans are somewhere down at the bottom of the totem pole. But our skin is gorgeous, and comes in so many deep hues." She firmly believes if she had had a doll like this as a child, it would have given her greater confidence. Dr. Lisa told Walmart she was on board.

Find your mission

She renamed her company World of EPI™, LLC (Entertainment, Publishing and Inspiration), with the mission to be an expression of joy. She further believed that this venture would be an avenue to promote her ministry of positive self-esteem. From concept to production, Positively Perfect™ Dolls took approximately two years to complete. While the process was extraordinary, it was by no means effortless. Dr. Lisa had no manufacturing or previous experience in the toy industry. "I had to master a steep a learning curve overnight," she says. "There was no other company I could go to for help. I was a researcher, so I learned and studied the business. In many ways my inexperience in the business was an asset, because I didn't know what couldn't be done. I was naive enough to think I could create a doll that was authentically beautiful even though I had no capital, no mentoring, and no team. My passion, drive, and strong desire had enabled me to be the first African American to graduate with a PhD in Logistics and Marketing from Ohio State. I was the first African

American woman to receive tenure at Penn State, the first woman to receive a multimillion endowed dollar chair, the first female full professor in my field. All of these empowered me to feel I could do anything, even if I didn't have experience," she says. "When you are the first, you are the trailblazer. You fall down, scrape your knees, then get up and continue on. That's what I did. I have several scrapes on my knees, so to speak. But I just rubbed the bruises and moved forward. In essence, after studying the business, I followed my heart and went about figuring out how to make this happen," she adds. Dr. Lisa learned to negotiate with suppliers, which proved difficult because she didn't have a reputation or years of experience in the business. She also learned that national retailers have very strict requirements and that all factories do not qualify. While maintaining her residency in San Diego, she traveled to China often to develop relationships with manufacturers there, even though she didn't speak the language. Despite being able to prove that she had a relationship with major retailers, she got no support from banks and had to use her own personal resources to get the business off the ground. Through it all, Dr. Lisa continued to stay focused. It was a labor of love.

Have Patience and Perseverance

At many points throughout the journey, Dr. Lisa wanted to give up, thinking it was all too hard, that she didn't have enough help or any of the other things that she didn't have or have access to. But at every point when she wanted to call it quits, she was reminded of why she needed to press on. Early on, the company wasn't making any money and eventually filed for bankruptcy. She estimates that she probably lost about $500,000 of her own personal funds. It was during these darkest hours that her faith and belief in what she was doing saw her through. "Despite the incredible losses we were suffering, I had an abiding faith that I would never be abandoned. My belief was that if I could quiet my negative thinking, I would be given insights and direction. I kept thinking of Nelson Mandela, Gandhi, and Martin Luther King. All these incredible souls looked out at the impossible but stayed connected to an inner possibility. They were led by an abiding faith that they could create a society based on love when the world reflected hate. I truly believed that if I could hold on to knowing that something bigger than me was orchestrating my life, then all would be well. I believe that if I start towards a goal where I can figure everything out, then the goal is too small. I have to reach further than I can see. I have to leave an opportunity for a Power bigger than me to appear. If my plan isn't a little scary, then it's not worthy of me; it's too small. It won't allow me to grow into who I was created to be," she says. Dr. Lisa indicated the biggest change she encountered was growing spiritually. "There is usually a solution to a business problem, but faith allows you to persevere when the solution is not readily available," she says.

Trust Your Instincts

When beginning the process to create the dolls, Dr. Lisa recalls, "I wanted to do something that honored our community and had a long-term positive impact on our race." Based on observing young women with low self-esteem in her college classrooms, Dr. Lisa made the connection that low self-esteem developed in early childhood, the time when girls were playing with dolls. With the Positively Perfect™ collection, through the intimate bond that girls have with their dolls, young girls of color would be able to see their own intelligence and beautiful selves (full lips and noses, deep eyes, custom-blended skin tones, and hairstyles worn by multicultural children) reflected back during positive playtime.

Despite having a partnership with Walmart, Dr. Lisa, like most small businesses, experienced her share of challenges when building her business—lack of finances/capital, lack of experience, lack of access to national advertising, to name a few. "Operating with a small team, we were all spread thin," recalls Dr. Lisa. Working through these challenges, Dr. Lisa grew the company from negative revenues into a multimillion-dollar powerhouse. World of EPI™ is now a leading multicultural toy manufacturing and design firm with a global supply chain that crisscrosses the world from the United States to China and other worldwide destinations. Since hitting the shelves, Positively Perfect™ Dolls have sold exceptionally well. "We began with two dolls in about 300 stores. They have become so successful, we have expanded into over 4,500 outlets in several national retail chains," says Dr. Lisa. Because the dolls are beautiful, with fun and joyful expressions, consumers often say they wish they had dolls like this growing up. She receives comments from customers from all over the world expressing their joy when they find the product online or in stores.

Dr. Lisa continues to look for ways to expand the brand, which has grown from infant dolls to include dolls for older girls and preteens. Her newest collection, the D.I.V.A.H. Collection (Dignified, Intelligent, Vivacious, Attractive, Humanitarian) represents how Dr. Lisa sees the girls who buy her dolls. Although this line appeals to an older child, Dr. Lisa is also proud of the fact that these dolls aren't sexy. "You'll never see them in a sexy outfit," asserts Dr. Lisa enthusiastically. They are confident and beautiful in ways beyond sexuality. One of the biggest and most obvious comparisons that Dr. Lisa's dolls receive is to the American Girl™ dolls. Although she understands the comparisons, Dr. Lisa says her dolls were not created to be compared with them. "The D.I.V.A.H. collection was designed to address a need in the market for a multicultural doll that we felt was not being met. We've been interviewed on a number of televions shows, in print articles, and on radio including MSNBC's *News Nation* with Tamron Hall, the *New York Times*, theGrio.com, *Black Enterprise Magazine*, Aspire network's *Exhale*, Forbes.com, MadameNoire.com, Bright House Network commercial, WABC's *Here and Now*, and *Café Mocha* – to talk about how multiculturalism is celebrated with our dolls, which is a testament to our core beliefs," says Dr. Lisa.

When asked to whom she can attribute her success and what drives her, Dr. Lisa says, "I attribute any success that I have attained to those who came before me. I stand on the shoulders of trailblazers and those courageous enough to try something that's never been done before. Those who had the foresight to look beyond the obvious and to see what's possible. I like to recall Nelson Mandela, Martin Luther King, and Gandhi, because they had an inner guidance that allowed them to be of service to others. They are examples of what one person can do when they allow themselves to be an instrument of something much bigger than themselves."

Dr. Lisa hopes that when she leaves this earth, she will have left behind a positive legacy and a child who feels beautiful. This thought is what drives her to get up every morning and hope that if one little girl looks in the mirror and is happy about who she is because she played with a Positively Perfect™ Doll, then she's done her work. Dr. Lisa strongly believes that "play" helps strengthen little girls to deal with life's issues. If they can find positive reinforcement in a toy, then hopefully those good thoughts— thoughts about themselves, and others—will transfer to their day-to-day thinking when it comes to their self-esteem. While she is deeply appreciative of her family and her talented team, she affirms that her heart most often leaps for joy when she sees and meets the smiling faces of beautiful children of all ethnicities. "Their excitement and hugs from their parents have inspired me to create authentic beautiful toys worthy of their intelligence and beauty," she adds.

50 Billion Dollar Boss Moves
When turning your idea into a business, you should:

- Let inspiration find you;
- Find your mission;
- Have patience and perseverance; and
- Trust your instincts.

CHAPTER 3

I *Think* I Love You: Branding Your Passion and Understanding Your Unique Value Proposition

Monif Clarke, Founder and CEO, Monif C. Plus Sizes

While many entrepreneurial ventures are started due to the desire to monetize a hobby or passion, some ventures are more opportunistic and are started because an individual sees a need in the market. And some are started because the individual just knows that they do not want to work for someone else forever but are not necessarily sure what they want to do. Regardless of how the entrepreneurial venture starts, finding and maintaining enjoyment, even when it is not always fun, can be a challenge. They say when you do something you love, you will never work again. The reality is more complicated than that. Understanding the value that your business brings to the market is a key element in determining whether your venture will be a success or a failure.

Monif Clarke is the Founder and CEO of Monif C. Plus Sizes, a contemporary plus-sized ready-to-wear clothing brand. Founded in 2005, Monif C. Plus Sizes is geared toward the fashion-savvy, modern-day plus-sized woman who desires clothing that fits her diverse lifestyle, whether it is business, travel, or leisure. Her business consists of 10 employees and comprises an e-commerce site, a boutique in Manhattan, and a wholesale business with retailers across the United States, London, Canada, Australia, Sweden, Jamaica, St. Maarten, the Bahamas, and Bermuda. Boasting annual sales of well over $1 million, Monif has been featured in *Crain's New York Business*, on Fox Business America's *Nightly Scoreboard*, on *The View*, on ABC News, and in *Glamour*, *InStyle*, and *Lucky* magazines and boasts partnerships with Ideeli, Overstock, One Stop Plus, and Sonsi. com, a subsidiary of Charming Shoppes, Zappos, and Nordstrom, to name a few. She was also a 2011 Black Enterprise Small Business Awards finalist. Monif tells her story of how she was able to brand and build a business around her passion and why "being her own customer" was the value proposition that she brought to the market. All of this has been the secret to her company's success.

A Starter Business

Following in her father's footsteps, Monif earned her BA in Math and Computer Science from Rutgers University. She had planned to start a nonprofit centered on getting children access to accelerated math/science education, and briefly worked at her alma mater. Increasingly feeling discontent with her chosen career path, however, Monif recalls her mother insisting, "You need to figure out a business—because you are meant to be a CEO!"

Monif would eventually heed these words. She and her mother became partners and started a business selling refurbished children's clothes that they found at Goodwill and consignment shops on eBay. She got a crash course in dealing with customers and quickly learned that moms were very specific about the clothes that they wanted for their children. They wanted brand names like Tommy Hilfiger and Ralph Lauren at a good price. She also learned that, because of the Internet, people were moving away from being solely dependent on department stores and their exorbitant prices, in order to get the goods that they wanted.

At the height of the business, Monif and her mother were making $30,000 a month. After just a year in business, they were awarded the prestigious Success in Small Business Award from the New Jersey Small Business Development Center.

Although the eBay business was successful, Monif was always on the search for new entrepreneurial ventures to develop. She pitched the idea of a cleaning business to her mother, but the venture lasted only a month. Although she was initially disappointed, it was a blessing in disguise, as little did she know this short-term setback and the lessons learned from her previous business would set the stage for her next big endeavor.

London's Calling

In 2005, Monif was on vacation in London visiting relatives. A cousin was in the fashion industry and took her along on a factory visit. Monif recalls, "When I walked in and saw the clothing, I immediately thought, wow, why doesn't someone design clothing like this for women my size?"

Her cousin replied, "Why don't you do it?"

Monif lamented there were not enough fashionable clothes available for plus-sized women. Monif recalls, "My mum didn't have an easy time dressing me. I figured if this is what I went through as a plus-sized woman, then imagine what others were going through." Monif always had an interest in designing clothes and at that moment, she thought the timing was right for her to become a clothing designer for plus-sized women. Always her biggest supporter, her mum encouraged her to go for it.

Monif flew home excited and eager to breathe life into this new idea. Despite having no formal fashion training, later that year, she launched Monif C. Plus Sizes. She and her mother both decided to quit the eBay business to start working on developing the clothing line. Monif then returned to England, where she spent a month at a factory learning everything she could about the clothing industry and how garments were made. "That experience was my crash course in fashion design," she said. As expected, it was not smooth sailing, as Monif and her mother traveled back and forth between New Jersey, where they were living, and New York, visiting garment factories and talking to everyone in the industry, down to those who made zippers and buttons.

Monif would pitch her design ideas to the major retailers, only to be told again and again that no one would purchase her clothing. "I heard every type of rejection there is: it's too trendy, too colorful, too sexy, and my favorite, plus-sized customers aren't fashion conscious," she says. Yet Monif knew these retailers were missing a huge untapped market. As a plus-size fashionable woman herself, Monif knew that plus-sized clothes could be glamorous, fashion forward, colorful, and flattering, all the things that every other woman wants in clothes.

Her competitors at the time believed that plus-size women want to hide their curves and troublesome areas, so what they offered was boxy, drab, and unflattering. Monif and her mother had many doors closed on them, but they were not discouraged. After being rejected by every big box retailer, "we decided to take a leap of faith and manufacture the product ourselves and hoped it would sell through our e-commerce site, Monifc.com," says Monif. "By going directly to the consumer, we really learned the intricacies of the business and built a tremendous customer base. Our customers are extremely loyal which has helped us show the potential of this market and get the attention of major retailers," she adds.

Now that she was going to manufacture on her own, Monif needed to find a production factory that could make her designs in large quantities so that she could sell them at a price at which she would actually make a profit. "Most of the domestic factories, especially those in New York City, manufacture small volumes or sample quantities. To really get your production costs down, you usually have to source from factories overseas," says Monif. After months of sourcing, she finally had a breakthrough when she attended a Coterie trade show and saw the line from Cary Marcus. Monif admits, she hounded Marcus every week for a month to get him to take her seriously. "I had pitched my idea to him, but he simply said to me, 'This is small change compared to what I do.'" Still not discouraged, she finally got the break she needed when Marcus gave her the names of some people he worked with in the business. "This was the break that I'd been looking for," says Monif. "To this day, I still maintain business ties with them," she adds.

Monif Is Her Own Customer

For Monif, selling to this customer is easy, because she *is* her customer. She likens the branding as telling her story and that of women like her—women who like fashionable clothes, and jetsetters who travel the world and *love* their curves., She knew that, like her, they did not want to be defined or relegated to covering up their size as if it were something to be ashamed of rather than embraced and celebrated.

When she first started the company, the plus-sized market was dominated by mall staples like Lane Bryant, Ashley Stewart, and Torrid. As she saw it, based on the offerings of these companies, the target customer was "a plus-sized middle-aged white woman in the Midwest." There's nothing wrong with that, but this was not how Monif saw herself, the women whom she knew, and millions of other plus-sized women. The big, established companies did not know how to talk to this market, and employed a broad-brush strategy of marketing to everyone. However, Monif knew that when you market to everyone, you market to no one.

Although she had a business background, she had no in-depth marketing and branding plan, and she relied heavily on her gut. She knew her philosophy would translate to the plus-sized market, and settled on a niche that she felt her competitors were not addressing. She specifically identified her consumer as aged 25 to 50, living in a major metropolitan area, who likes fashion-forward clothes and is willing to pay for them. While it sounds like this could be the customer for any product targeting women, the fundamental difference was that, as far as Monif could see, no one seemed to be selling and speaking to women who were all of these things and who also happened to be plus-sizedd.

Long before it was fashionable, Monif began to use models who were actually plus sized, rather than using models who were size ten or twelve and calling them plus sized. Monif portrayed this customer the way they saw themselves—sexy, contemporary, and fashion forward. She specifically avoided copy that promoted the standard ideas of coverage, slimming, or anything that de-emphasized the body. One of the first key models for Monif C was Mia Amber Davis-Yard, a producer, actress and popular plus sized model. "I vividly remember her bright spark, poise and confidence—everything that we believed the Monif C customer embodied. She was a Monif C fan before she was our model," says Monif. "Size diversity is key for us. We believe that every woman of size can wear Monif C, and that's a key element in our branding and marketing strategy. Furthermore, not every model we've used was first signed to a big agency. We've grown with a few of our models and we like their diversity in size, height, race and ethnicity," adds Monif.

Her approach was a breath of fresh air and different than anything that had ever been presented. When she would get flack that the models were too big, she would insist, "This is what our customer looks like."

She also found that she is the company's best marketing tool. "Our marketing strategy includes partnering with vendors that cater to our target market and heavy utilization of social media." Although it started out as a way to stay engaged with current customers, YouTube has been a tremendous way for them to introduce the brand to new customers who may never have heard of them. "We would create videos of myself showcasing our collections, which we would shoot in our showroom with customers trying on the clothing so women can see them on different shapes and sizes. The original objective was to get existing customers to buy more frequently or alerting them about new items by sending them an e-mail, telling them to go watch the YouTube video, then go to Monifc.com to shop. We found that when women went to YouTube to search for 'plus-sized clothing' or 'plus-sized swimsuits,' they found our videos, which made them want to visit the site, where they usually made a purchase," she adds.

Monif C. Plus Sizes quickly became known as the brand that actually used real plus-sized models in marketing. This was a first and made them distinctive within the industry. As imitation is the biggest form of flattery, she soon found that people were watching and taking notes.

Consultants Do Not Always Know What's Best for Your Brand

Although the landscape changed tremendously after Monif first started, there was still a lot of work to do. Showing a plus-sized woman as sexy, contemporary, fashion forward, and owning the room were concepts that were foreign to this market. She found that, despite the success that she had achieved, there were those who still wanted to discount the viability of the market and this consumer.

As she looked to grow her brand, she sought expertise from consultants. She understood as a business, some extensions made sense, but she was not prepared for the suggestions that the consultants tried to steer her toward. She heard suggestions to tone down the colors and use more neutrals—grey, tan, and other boring shades; incorporate sizes four to twenty-four rather than just fourteen to twenty-four; or create more career wear and work separates. Monif felt that these approaches were contrary to her customer base and would not reflect what her customer wanted and looked to her for. She finally found that making adjustments to the clothes in response to what the consumers wanted was the best path. She continues to work to stay above the fray and steer the brand in the direction that has made her successful and not succumb to outside pressure. Today, the plus size market is one of the fastest growing consumer segments in the apparel industry. According to NPD Group, as of April 2014 sales revenue generated was $17.5 billion; a 5% increase from the prior year, and up just over a billion dollars from the $16.4 billion recorded three years ago.

Every Opportunity Is Not an Opportunity for You

Monif recalls one experience that should have been an exciting meeting turned into eye-opening experience. At an important meeting with a female investment banker who happened to be African American, the banker suggested Monif incorporate more diversity into her ads. Specifically, she suggested that Monif consider a popular, older, and more conservative Caucasian actress as a spokesperson. This advice was a shock, to say the least. Monif remained very deliberate in her response, and replied that she could not imagine that this actress, whom she was sure was a perfectly lovely woman, would be the least bit interested in wearing Monif's clothes, and that the actress did not represent Monif's target audience. She further adds, "I could not even begin to understand the customer that this actress could speak to."

Seek Out Defining Moments That Make Sense for the Brand and Your Target Audience

As a fashion brand, Monif knew that people needed to *see* the brand. In the early days, she spent a lot of time sending out press kits to editors. As the press started to take notice, she was frequently called upon to send samples to magazines when they were in need of clothes for plus-sized models. She became the "it" brand for magazines doing fashion spreads featuring plus-sized women because they knew they would get fashion-forward clothes. She started fielding calls from magazines such as *InStyle, Glamour,* and *Marie Claire.*

But it was a call from *Essence* magazine that really changed the trajectory of the business. In the spring of 2012, the magazine was preparing for a photo shoot featuring Jill Scott, the Grammy award-winning R&B singer and actress. Unbeknownst to Monif at the time, the spread featured Jill in four different outfits wearing only Monif's clothes. After that issue was published, Monif admits she was caught off guard by the effects that followed, as sales that year doubled. While this was a good problem to have, it required her to ramp up unbudgeted resources, inventory, and production very quickly. While she cannot attribute this increase in sales solely to that shoot, without a doubt, it was a big part of it.

The other exposure that occurred was on television. If you think you have seen Monif on television before, you are right. Monif C. Plus Sizes has been featured on Black Entertainment Television's (BET's) highly popular show *Rip the Runway*, which featured cutting-edge brands by designers of color, not just once but *five* times, which Monif thinks might be a record. She recalls the first time she got the call to appear. She knew this would be an exciting opportunity and, in many ways, the first introduction to many customers around the world who had never heard of the Monif C. Plus Sizes brand. True to her advertising and branding, she featured actual plus-sized women, embracing their curves and gliding down the runway. She also did something that had *never* been done before: feature plus-sized women wearing bikinis! The response was phenomenal, with her website ultimately crashing. Monif and her clothes are now regularly featured on shows such as *The Today Show* and *What Not to Wear,* to name a few.

Become the "Champion" for Your Brand

With the success and visibility that Monif has achieved, she is now at the stage where she is considering investor funding in order to move her company to the next phase, which includes continuing to grow the e-commerce business, opening more retails stores and getting wider distribution from national chains. She is also working to fill key senior management positons. "There was a time when I was doing everything myself, shipping boxes, doing my own PR, picking up rolls of fabric from vendors just to save money on freight, and anything else I could do myself" she says. "Although it was great to bootstrap in the beginning because it saved a lot of money, there comes a time when you have to hire staff so you can better manage your time and use it to work on growing your business, not just putting out daily fires. I realized this model of me doing everything was not sustainable as I looked to grow my company," she adds.

As an outsider to influential networks and lacking the "pedigree" of many of her contemporaries who have the benefit of relationships from business school or even prep school, Monif finds herself having to work harder to go into meetings and get to the table based on the strength of what she has created. But she is committed to her brand and telling the story—and she has trouble taking "no" for an answer.

Her ability to articulate her story and champion her brand has garnered her invitations to take advantage of exposure to investor events and garner warm introductions to influencers, where, sadly, she sees a lot of faces that do not look like hers—namely, African American women. Having witnessed the advantages and the impact these relationships have had on her business, she wishes more of her peers had access to these networks.

She also counts experts such as Lisa Price, Founder and CEO of Carol's Daughter (now a part of L'Oreal USA) as a mentor, who advises her on all aspects of the business from scaling to funding and just being a sounding board. "She's been an amazing mentor. I've been blessed to have her help guide me, and she has been very vocal about some of her own pitfalls, which is helping me to become a better businesswoman," says Monif.

Having bootstrapped her company herself, taking profits and reinvesting them back into the business, she boasts revenues in the seven figures and is especially protective of what she has built. She has made it to the big leagues on her own terms, and people are happy to see her.

50 Billion Dollar Boss Moves

There are riches in the niches. To brand your passion and understand your unique value proposition, you should:

- Realize consultants do not always know what is best for your brand;
- Remember that every opportunity is not an opportunity for you;
- Seek out defining moments that make sense for the brand and your target audience; and
- Become the "champion" for your brand.

CHAPTER 4

Who Do I Run to? Finding a Mentor and Building Mentor Relationships

Yolanda H. Caraway, Founder and CEO, The Caraway Group

Increasingly, it is becoming less of a surprise to see African Americans in positions of power as business owners or company executives. Despite these achievements, though, many women lament the difficulty in finding and establishing mentor relationships. The ability to establish relationships tends to be hampered due to the executive's increased responsibilities and limited time to perform in those roles. Often, unless you are privy to these circles, there is a lack of knowledge that these women even hold these positions of influence and power. Further, many people have "mentor vision," in that they have a specific vision for what their mentor will look like, how the relationship will develop, and the role the mentor will play. In reality, mentor relationships can take many forms, including formal or informal; career, company, or industry specific; or long standing or short term, to name a few.

Yolanda H. Caraway is Founder and CEO of The Caraway Group, a boutique public relations agency located in Washington DC. Since founding The Caraway Group in 1987, Yolanda and her team have counseled well-known Fortune 500 companies, nonprofit organizations, government agencies, and high-profile individuals in every aspect of communications strategy. She is a nationally recognized public relations and public affairs strategist who is known for policy-making, political management, and public relations work in government, and nonprofit and private sectors. She has worked with major US companies such as Microsoft Corporation, Google, AT&T, MGM Mirage, Bristol Myers Squibb, Mitsubishi, and Texaco.

Additionally, for the past three decades, Yolanda has played a major role in shaping the goals and objectives of the national Democratic Party, and has been called upon throughout her career to coordinate various party efforts. Her agency has counseled government and nonprofit agencies such as the Congressional Black Caucus Foundation, the Congressional Hispanic Caucus Institute, the US Department of Commerce, the Annie E. Casey Foundation, the Center for American Progress, and events such as the NATO Fiftieth Anniversary Summit, the NAACP Image Awards, the Martin Luther King Jr. National Memorial Foundation Project, and the Fiftieth Anniversary of the March on Washington.

In 2009, Yolanda was appointed to the Council on American Politics, a group of nationally renowned political leaders addressing current affairs and working toward the growth and enrichment of The George Washington University School of Political Management. Yolanda is a member of the Corporate Directors Group and the American College of Corporate Directors, and serves on the board of directors of the Washington Performing Arts Society.

In the pages that follow, she shares how she has benefited from numerous mentor relationships over her many years in business and politics, and how she pays this forward to upcoming public relations professionals.

Rising Star

Yolanda grew up in Rochester, New York. Perhaps unlike most children, she had an early interest in entrepreneurship and politics. She fondly recalls her early entrepreneurial ventures—having a lemonade stand, helping her father who owned a janitorial company, or selling Amway when she was just 12. She had her first taste of politics came when she was just 14 years old. President John F. Kennedy had been assassinated the year before. His brother, Bobby Kennedy, had launched a campaign for the US Senate in New York State. A friend encouraged her to volunteer for the campaign. While other ninth graders were thinking about the "firsts" of high school, Yolanda took the bus across town every day to campaign headquarters to do whatever needed to be done. She folded letters, stuffed envelopes, made phone calls, and did anything else she was asked to do. Bobby Kennedy won the election, and she received a letter from him thanking her for her service—a letter that still hangs in her office today. That was it for her. "The excitement and exhilaration was beyond anything I had ever experienced in my life. I knew politics was where I wanted to be," says Yolanda.

Her first big national break came when she was hired to work for Congresswoman Barbara Mikulski (D-MD) (recently retired US Senator). This was after she had spent time working for Xerox Corporation, where she knew she would not make a career.

Seven months later, right after President Jimmy Carter had lost his bid for re-election, Ann Lewis, the congresswoman's chief of staff who had hired Yolanda, went to work for the Democratic National Committee (DNC) as political director. She asked Yolanda if she would be interested in joining her, and of course she was. "This experience was invaluable because I felt like I was finally on the path to creating the career that I wanted," she explains.

In her new role, she was the director of education and training for candidates around the country. She learned how to put together training seminars, and manage and promote them, and she learned how to handle VIP clients and guests. It was around this time that Yolanda began to think about possibly owning her own business one day. Always keeping an eye toward this goal, she started meeting influential people who might be vital when she decided to start her own company. Over the years, she also worked on numerous campaigns, including a few presidential campaigns. At the end of each campaign, she started noticing a trend. During each campaign, she worked alongside many white men. She knew that she was just as smart and competent as they (and in many cases, more so), but the big difference was that they had two key advantages: more *experience* and more *access*. They knew how to use the campaign and the relationships that they had developed to start their own successful businesses, and she felt there was no reason that she could not do the same and start her own firm and be successful.

Political Insider

In 1984, after taking a leave of absence from the DNC to work on the Mondale-Ferraro general election campaign, Yolanda met Reverend Jesse Jackson, who had just made his first presidential run. After the election, she went back to the DNC, when after several months she received a call from Reverend Jackson asking her to come work for him and help put his next campaign in place. She went to work as his chief of staff, and during that time she traveled around the country and, as she says, "met probably every black elected official in office at that time." Although she was working for Reverend Jackson, she knew she was gaining invaluable contacts that she would use one day. When the campaign was over, she continued to keep in touch with people whom she had met, whether through a quick call, a personal note or, when possible, meeting for lunch or dinner. "Washington, DC is all about connections. When you don't stay in touch, people forget about you," she says. By this time, the entrepreneurial urge was getting stronger. While she was not quite ready to fully make the leap, she knew that it was eventually going to happen. Anticipating this time, in 1987 she incorporated her business, the Caraway Group.

While still working her day job, her new company began picking up work on the side through partnering with the late Caroline Jones of Caroline Jones Advertising. Caroline was an African American businesswoman and pioneer in the advertising industry. She started her career with the J. Walter Thompson Company and was the first African American woman elected vice president of a major advertising agency. Caroline died of cancer in 2001.

One of her former colleagues from the DNC was the late Ron Brown who, at the time, was a partner in the law firm of Patton, Boggs and Blow. This became a critical relationship for Yolanda as he was once a rising star on the political scene and he wanted to get back into Democratic politics in a major way. Yolanda suggested that he join the 1988 campaign as convention manager, in charge of Reverend Jackson's convention operation. With Yolanda's help, he went on to become the first African American chairman of a major political party. He appointed her his senior adviser, and she managed the site-selection process for the 1992 national convention. Brown went on to become President Bill Clinton's secretary of commerce, once again becoming the first African American to hold that position. Tragically, he died in a plane crash in 1996. "We genuinely helped each other. I'll always remember that this relationship helped propel me to the national stage," she says.

Time to Make a Move

Yolanda finally felt the time was right to devote her attentions to her company, The Caraway Group. "I had worked for the DNC for nearly 20 years," says Yolanda, "and had key contacts around the country. I certainly didn't think getting work would be a problem, but it was at that time that I learned my most valuable lesson," she adds. Thinking the phone was going to ring off the hook with offers of business, she was more than taken aback when no one called. Incredulous, she could not fathom that after all of her years of dedication to the Democratic Party, no one was thinking about her. She recalls that, early on, she knew that she wanted and frankly "expected" one of her "friends" who now ran the government to be helpful in identifying business opportunities for her firm, but, admittedly, she did not know what to ask for. "Once President Clinton was in the White House, it was an exciting time," she says. "It was the first time that African Americans were really able to come to the table as contractors and be thought of as real entrepreneurs and not just an afterthought when they needed money or votes. It was also the first time that you saw real diversity in office, so the opportunities and potential became endless."

It was at that moment that she knew she had to *learn what she wanted and what to ask for*. "This is how the white men in the established business culture had done it," she says. "They knew, and if they didn't, someone would call them. We didn't have those options."

With conviction, and using her new insights, Yolanda worked to identify opportunities that would be good for her business. She then reached out to the extensive network that she had cultivated throughout the years, first, to tell them that she now had her own firm and, second, to find the appropriate contacts. She then began campaigns to secure the business. This strategy worked, and within months, she started picking up several clients, and her business began to take off. "I wasn't selected for every project that I went after, but I won enough to keep us busy, and through some of these relationships, we started to pick up corporate clients, says Yolanda.

Her firm started out in event planning, then grew into public relations when she picked up Microsoft as a client. "Although I started out in politics and found a niche in this industry when I went to work for myself, Caroline Jones became a business mentor," says Yolanda. "Her mentorship was invaluable as she taught me everything about business. She even taught me how to write my first invoices," Yolanda fondly recalls. She soon picked up other Fortune 500 companies, including MGM Mirage and AT&T. At its peak, her firm earned revenues of $5 million. Everything was going well until 2008, when the economy crashed. Like everyone else at the time, she was forced to downsize—"Unfortunately, not soon enough," she says. Her firm did recover and the business is now exactly the right size as she considers new projects and moves into the next phase of her career.

Think Outside the "Ideal" Mentor Box

Yolanda recalls that she had the benefit of working with, and having, mentors of different races, genders, and industries. She says these relationships were ideal in that these individuals were more experienced than she, and her association with them allowed her to glean as much insight as possible. "I did not always seek mentors, but I was fortunate to have working relationships that often turned into mentor relationships. They saw that I listened and was willing to learn from them. This, in turn, made them want to share information with me," says Yolanda. "Had I not been open to receiving input from someone else, I might have missed this opportunity to learn from knowledgeable and well-respected leaders," explains Yolanda.

Have Several Mentors

Yolanda recalls several people who were very instrumental in all stages of her career. Her first mentor was Ann Lewis, who became her political mentor. She credits her with giving her one of her first opportunities in national politics. "Although I worked behind the scenes, she taught me how the political game *really* works," says Yolanda.

Her next mentor, Caroline Jones, became her business mentor and taught her everything about business, from providing practical advice to how to negotiate a deal. They went on to start a business together, CCS Events, which was formed around the 1992 Democratic Convention in New York City.

Another mentor, the late Ron Brown, helped propel her to the national stage. She has been involved in every national convention since 1984 and, most recently, managed the backstage and podium operations for the 2008 and 2012 Democratic National Conventions.

Realize Every Relationship Has Potential

Once she decided that she wanted to open a business, Yolanda approached business dealings with an eye toward the future. With every opportunity that came her way, Yolanda completed it with her future business in mind. Business acquaintances became potential business clients. Colleagues became potential partners. "Every situation became a prospect," says Yolanda. When the timing was right and she decided to focus on her own business, she was able to leverage those relationships to secure contracts and propel her business.

Create a Reputation Worthy of Mentorship

Yolanda earned a reputation as a go-to person to get things done. After nearly 20 years, she had attained leadership roles within the DNC and been able to successfully leverage relationships that always led to her next opportunity, whether within the committee, on national campaigns, or through her own agency. "While I am sure I would have been successful, I'm not sure how long it would have taken my firm to achieve the level of success that it has experienced. Having the mentor relationships that I've had, changed the direction of my business in many ways and definitely shortened the learning curve for me," says Yolanda.

50 Billion Dollar Boss Moves
Attracting and building mentor relationships can be challenging. To attract the right mentors to help you and your business, you should:

- Think outside the "ideal" mentor box;
- Have several mentors;
- Realize every relationship has potential; and
- Create a reputation worthy of mentorship.

CHAPTER 5

Adding Value: Building Mutually Beneficial Strategic Partnerships

Dana Hill, Founder and CEO, Cocotique

In today's business environment, it is almost impossible to successfully go it alone. Building a foundation through strategic partnerships is advantageous for any enterprise. However, for small businesses, it can be a critical component to their success and longevity. Regardless of the size of the enterprise, ideal partnerships are mutually beneficial in that both parties can gain an advantage by the alliance. Unfortunately, many small businesses do not seek out partnerships as they underestimate the value that they can bring to a large corporation due to their short amount of time in business or their limited experience. Understanding the needs and objectives of the potential partner and how you can help them fulfill that need, and vice versa, can ensure partnerships that are robust and set up for success.

Dana Hill is the Founder and CEO of Cocotique, a deluxe beauty box subscription company for women of color. Launched in 2013, Cocotique is a digital beauty platform that delivers the best in beauty and lifestyle products to subscribers each month. From skin care, fragrances, and makeup, to hair care and lifestyle categories, Cocotique curates an assortment of products that appeal to women of color. The "Cocotique Experience" comes full circle with an online magazine that not only features an in-depth look inside the brands in the box, expert tips, and tutorials but also provides subscribers with informative articles on beauty, health, fitness, fashion, and entertainment.

Partnerships are imperative for a business like Dana's. She shares her story of how she has been able to leverage previous relationships to establish strategic partnerships that have been advantageous for everyone involved.

A Thriving Career

Dana received a BBA degree in Marketing from the American College in London, where she graduated magna cum laude. She began her career in the fashion industry as an assistant market editor in the fashion department at *Vogue* magazine, and later moved to *Harper's Bazaar* magazine as an assistant fashion editor. She then transitioned into public relations and marketing when she headed up the PR/marketing department for Phat Farm for six years and was instrumental in the launch of the Baby Phat brand. As vice president of marketing and PR for Phat Farm, and later as vice president of marketing for Rocawear and Eve's clothing line Fetish, she designed and implemented numerous integrated marketing, PR, event, and advertising programs that increased brand visibility, market presence, and sales.

Dana's experience outside of the fashion industry includes serving as senior director of artist development at Arista Records, where she gained invaluable entertainment industry experience. She also spearheaded the development of GA1's public relations department, a marketing and advertising firm in Maryland. She was responsible for overseeing the day-to-day activities of the public relations and marketing department, including media outreach, strategic partnerships, and the development of communications plans for its clients in the government, health-care, nonprofit, hospitality, and consumer products sectors.

Entrepreneur in the Making

Prior to launching Cocotique, Dana founded the Divine Marketing Group, a boutique public relations, strategic marketing, special events, and luxury gifting consultancy specializing in fashion, jewelry, beauty, and lifestyle brands. Divine Marketing Group provided communications, gift bag production, event production, brand management, and strategic marketing services to fashion, beauty, jewelry, restaurant, and lifestyle clients. In 2002, Dana was featured in *Honey* magazine as one of "25 Women Making it Happen."

Going Out on Her Own

Dana started her business after working for other people, building widely recognized and celebrated brands for many years. Like most entrepreneurs, she wanted to be in a position where she was in control of her destiny. She had successfully helped several companies grow into thriving, global entities, and knew that if she applied the same dedication and drive to her own business, she could have the same level of success.

While there were other companies similar to Cocotique, Dana realized that few beauty brands catered to or addressed the beauty needs of women of color. With her extensive beauty background, she saw a need in the marketplace, and after thoroughly researching the competitive landscape, she started Cocotique in April 2012. "I began building the website in January and launched the social media platforms a month later to start building our social media presence. By getting a head start with our social media, it helped to start laying the foundation for the company. By using this strategy, we already had a healthy social media following when we launched the website and shipped the first box in August of that year," says Dana. "In fact, we were able to secure several beauty brands who learned about us from our social media presence," she adds.

Choose Partnerships That Create Value

Starting a business is no small feat, especially for a business like hers in which the market is still in its infancy. Dana knew that her business would be heavily dependent on partnerships, but strategic partnerships only work when both parties benefit. Having spent years in the beauty and urban markets, Dana had amassed an impressive network of contacts, connections, and potential strategic partners. However, she had to carefully assess these business relationships and identify those that would best align with her business model. She had to look at every angle of both her business and the partnering business to determine the greatest opportunities for partnership and growth. She determined the best partnerships were those that presented a mutually beneficial opportunity for both companies to increase their capabilities with an alliance. Open communication between both companies would be essential for a successful association and to maximize the synergies to the fullest. "I tried to target companies that would best align with my business model—a beauty centric, e-commerce company targeting women of color," says Dana.

In order to create the most value, she had to first determine what her company's and the other company's strengths were, and then figure out how their respective businesses complemented each other. With an end goal of better serving her customers by offering new services or products that she could not have done on her own, one of the first strategic partnerships she was able to develop was with *Hype Hair* magazine, the #1 beauty source for African American women. They created a quarterly Hype Hair + Cocotique Box, and offered subscribers a free digital subscription to *Hype Hair* magazine. This helped her create a distinct competitive advantage because no other subscription box had an alliance with a print publication.

Because of her past relationships, the first boxes Cocotique shipped were filled mostly with products from companies that she had worked with in the past or those where she knew the owner of the company. "I developed a deck that outlined the benefits of targeting my demographic and how we could help their brands gain more awareness and sales. After creating a target list of potential brand partners, I e-mailed them the deck and we either discussed in person or on the phone how we could work together," recalls Dana. "Early on, I did hear 'no,' but once they understood the business model and the potential of this market, they were willing to give us a shot. Our assortment of products has gotten much deeper, which is a testament to our success in delivering customers to our clients," she adds.

Early on, the focus was on building equity and credibility by featuring well-known companies. Knowing how critical the Internet was to the beauty industry and the success of her business model, she also started working with beauty bloggers before the actual launch. She featured a different "COCOBlogger" of the week leading up to a launch on social media. This foundation enabled Cocotique to grow at a much faster rate, and these alliances gave the company a competitive advantage and access to a wider range of expertise and resources. "There is no doubt that these partnerships gave our brand more equity and differentiation from our competitors," said Dana. "It has been a great benefit to have strong strategic partnerships and allies to help grow Cocotique."

Study the Industry... Yours and Your Partners

Before seeking to establish partnerships, Dana knew her industry, her company, and the value that she brought. She sought out those partners who had a specific need to fill and determined how she could fill it for them. She studied not only her strengths and weaknesses but those of her partners, and sought to develop a plan to help them overcome their weaknesses by capitalizing on her strengths and vice versa. "To have a successful alliance, it is essential that the partnership be mutually beneficial to both entities," she says. "The best partnerships are when each partner has strengths in different areas and the combination of the two results in a bigger whole. Generally, the more collaborative the partnership or alliance, the more successful the endeavor is. By bringing a shared vision and strong core values to the table, coupled with passion and dedication, you have a great start to forming an alliance that creates value," she adds.

Leverage Partnerships to Expand Your Reach and Lower Costs

While she had extensive relationships, Dana knew that as a start-up she could not have the impact that she wanted and that the product warranted without additional assistance. In addition to the subscribers she was able to secure prior to launching Cocotique, by developing the strategic partnership with her first partner, *Hype Hair*, she was also able to leverage their database of subscribers at no cost to her. In return, *Hype Hair* was now able to present their subscribers with a new product offering, which helped further solidify their positioning as a beauty destination for women of color.

Small businesses can benefit from strategic partnerships by the decreased costs associated with shared resources for marketing, advertising, tech, and other business areas. Dana's ability to leverage this relationship was instrumental in her overall marketing strategy to quickly establish Cocotique as a leader in the beauty industry.

Use Your Network

Dana's early experience at Phat Farm working alongside Russell Simmons, who could only be described as one of the preeminent entrepreneurs of our time, proved to be as incredible an experience as it was invaluable. She easily considers him an phenomenal mentor and a positive influence. Her working closely beside him had a huge influence on her as she observed and absorbed what it took to grow a company, as well as how to effectively manage multiple aspects of running a business. "No job is ever too big or too small," says Dana. "It's all about getting it done by any means necessary in a smart, efficient way."

Now that she has gotten past the start-up stage, she has assembled a strong network of advisers, most notably Len Burnett, Co-CEO and Group Publisher of Uptown Media Group and former Group Publisher of *Vibe Magazine*. Each individual provides critical insights and help as she prepares to raise funding to take her company to the next level and bring her luxury beauty boxes to women of color everywhere.

50 Billion Dollar Boss Moves

To develop strategic partnerships that add value and are mutually beneficial, you should:

- Choose partnerships that create value;
- Study the industry...yours and your potential partner's;
- Leverage partnerships to expand your reach and lower costs; and
- Use your network.

CHAPTER 6

Your Network Is Your Net Worth:
Building Your Relationship Currency

Melinda Emerson, the "SmallBizLady," President, Quintessence Group

The Internet, and specifically social media, has unquestionably changed the way entrepreneurs do business. In many ways it has disrupted the traditional model of business, allowing companies to connect immediately with their consumers, become more responsive to opportunities and threats in the market, and drive and grow business. It has become a way of networking by allowing people to develop and grow their business networks faster and more efficiently online. While the traditional model of networking- going to events, passing out cards, and hoping to make that vital connection -still works, social media is now a critical element of networking that cannot be ignored. Social media platforms such as Facebook, LinkedIn, YouTube, Twitter, and Instagram have taken the traditional networking model one step further, allowing savvy participants to connect to, literally, hundreds or thousands of contacts in a relatively short amount of time. Social media also allows companies to continually interact with their contacts to develop long-standing relationships. While nothing beats face-to-face, personal interaction, especially in business, social media has elevated this model, increasing the likelihood that you are meeting people who are interested and engaged in what you are talking about.

The next question becomes, now that I have all of these "friends" and "followers," how do I maximize this network to grow my business?

With the largest and longest running weekly chats on Twitter, reaching over 3 million followers each week, Melinda F. Emerson, also known as the Small Biz Lady, is considered America's number one small business expert. She has been a thriving entrepreneur for over 16 years, and is an internationally known keynote speaker. A pioneer in social media marketing, she is the creator and host of #Smallbizchat, the longest running live chat on Twitter for small business owners. In addition to being a former columnist for the *New York Times*, she is frequently quoted by the *Wall Street Journal*, *Fortune* magazine, MSNBC, and Fox News. *Forbes* magazine named her the number one woman for entrepreneurs to follow on Twitter.

Melinda is an expert on what it takes to successfully start a small business, marketing pitfalls to avoid, and how to become a brand in demand using social media. She is the publisher of her resource blog, www.succeedasyourownboss.com, which is syndicated by the *Huffington Post*, and is the best-selling author of *Become Your Own Boss in 12 Months* and the e-book *How to Become a Social Media Ninja*. Her latest book, *Become Your Own Boss in 12 Months*, 2nd edition, was released in January 2015.

Her company advises Fortune 500 companies including Pitney Bowes, American Express, Dell, Staples, Sam's Club, Chase Bank, Facebook, FedEx, Ikea, Verizon, Wells Fargo, and Xerox on how to create a path to purchase with entrepreneurs and women business owners.

She shares her story of how she was able to grow and cultivate a network to take her business to unimaginable heights.

Following in Oprah's Footsteps

It was during her sophomore year in college that Melinda really began to study Oprah Winfrey as a business role model for what she thought she might like to do. Oprah had the number one talk show in the county, had just opened Harpo Studios in Chicago, and was starting to produce original programming. Melinda saw Oprah as the first media personality to transition to entrepreneur, which put the seed of entrepreneurship in her head. Upon graduating from Virginia Tech, Melinda went back home and accepted a position as an associate producer with the local NBC affiliate in Pittsburgh.

After working there for a year, she moved to the NBC affiliate in Philadelphia. She stayed there for two years before moving across the street to the ABC affiliate, where she remained for two more years.

As she prepared to work over yet another Christmas, she began to rethink her career choice. She realized she had worked every major holiday for the previous five years and was putting in over 60 hours a week, rendering her personal life null and void. The newsrooms were hostile environments, and she always seemed to have bosses who were not supportive, especially the other black managers. She also felt that as a black woman, there was very little upward mobility for her. It was at this moment that she crafted her exit plan and started studying all aspects of the business.

In the spring of 1998, while still working for ABC, she started Quintessence Multimedia, a small video production company that developed product launch videos for corporations and patient education and outreach videos for hospitals. "My off days from the station were Mondays and Tuesdays, so it gave me time to work my business while still getting a paycheck," said Melinda. In early 1999, she left television news to pursue her business full time. As technology changed, she realized her clients were uploading the videos to their websites, so she expanded her services and started doing web development in addition to video production.

In 2000, she entered a citywide business plan competition, which she did not win. She entered again in 2001, and this time she won. She received $25,000 and free office space for a year, and hired her first employee. Within a year, she got her first contract with a major corporation. She poured everything she had into the business: "In my mind, I convinced myself that *no one* would outwork me and my team. I created a workaholic culture in my business," says Melinda. Their hard work paid off, and they were named number 29 on Philadelphia's list of 100 fastest-growing companies. She expanded her team and hired more employees. Her husband left his corporate job with General Electric and joined the business full time. "My company was on the move. We started getting national media attention and corporate contracts, which was great," she adds.

It All Falls Apart

By 2005, Melinda and her husband were expecting their first child. Shortly after discovering the pregnancy, her doctor determined she was high risk and put her on bed rest. While anticipating the birth of her first baby should have been a joyous occasion, it was far from it. "I created a culture in my business where I made all the key decisions and dealt with all the clients. Even though I had eight employees, my business couldn't run without me," she said. While she was absent from her business, it started falling apart. With technology not being what it is now (wi-fi was not yet available in homes there were no ipads, and she was using a Palm III smartphone), she was unable to manage the day-to-day operations, which she had been accustomed to doing. "It was a nightmare. I went from being a seven-day-a-week workaholic, to not being able to leave my house or even raise my voice for fear of hurting my baby. It was a terrifying time."

This inability to manage from her bedside left her plenty of time to think. She realized she had made a lot of mistakes building her business. She also realized how inefficient her staff was when she really needed them. Melinda recalled, "My employees would do whatever I asked, but no one took the initiative to keep things afloat while I was out." She also realized how much of a workaholic she had become. Before becoming pregnant, it was nothing for her to work 12 hours a day, take calls late into the night, or work through the weekends. She also expected her employees to have the same dedication that she did. "I would always buy lunch and dinner for my staff because I did not want them to leave. You could call my office at 8 p.m. and my full team would be there like it was 3 o'clock in the afternoon," she said. For her business, she had sacrificed having a life. She had few personal relationships outside of work. She realized she was successful and had achieved her professional goals, but at what cost?

Reflecting on this and all of the expensive lessons that she had learned while building her business, Melinda started writing down her experiences, and new ideas she had about running a successful business. She realized she would have run her business differently if she had had better advice. "Bed rest was literally and figuratively the best medicine," she said. "It forced me to stop and change everything about myself and my way of thinking. I am so grateful for that experience."

She knew she needed to reinvent her brand and her life.

Once her son was born, it was like she was reborn, and for the first time, she dreaded going back to the business. "Once I looked at his face, the love that I felt for my business literally vanished and went to my son," she recalls. "I no longer loved my business and didn't want to do it anymore." But now she had a family who was depending on her. Melinda recalls, "I had figure out how I was going to reinvent Quintessence with a business model that would allow me to work smarter, not harder."

At Age 33, a Midlife Crisis

Melinda was just 33 years old when she had what she called her midlife crisis. With the exception of her son, she was unhappy in every aspect of her life. Her marriage was on its last legs, her business was crashing, and her baby was dealing with some minor health problems. Although she went to church, she realized she did not have a regular prayer life. With encouragement from her pastor, she began praying regularly. Within three months, she got a vision in a dream three times. She then understood what she was called to do. She was going to become America's number one small business expert.

She realized everything she had done until now had prepared her for her next stage. After evaluating the most valuable aspects of her business, she concluded that what held the most value for her were the lessons that she had learned from running her business.

"I just had to figure out how to bottle up those hard-learned lessons and sell them," she said.

Working Smarter, Not Harder

While Melinda was working to grow her business, it required all of her time, energy, and focus. After having her son, and her business almost going under without her, she knew she needed to transition her model and rebuild her business and her brand in a way that allowed her to leverage what she had learned in her previous efforts. Most importantly, she needed a business that provided a work/life balance so that she could be with and enjoy her new son. When she returned to work, she set about putting her plans into action.

Strive to Build Relationships That Are More Than Just Transactional

One of Melinda's first tasks—a difficult one—was to lay off everyone, including her husband. She turned to her network to contract services that she needed.

She started doing personal coaching for small businesses. While coaching a client, she happened to advise them on a specific brand of business plan software that she liked, but unfortunately the software was difficult to find. She decided to call the company to find out where she could find it or order it. Somehow, she ended up talking to Peter Archer (who would go on to edit both her first and second books) and proceeded to complain about the fact that she could not find the product anywhere. She even offered suggestions on how they could improve the product. After listening patiently, he advised her that, like many companies do, they had removed the software because they were trying to figure out what they wanted to do with the brand, which was named after Bob Adams, the former head of the company. He said that they would not rerelease it unless they had some sort of book to accompany it.

Seizing this opportunity, Melinda quickly replied, "Well, I have a book."

Peter asked her about her book and who was going to publish it. While Melinda's "book" really consisted of a few chapters and notes that she had written while on bed rest, she told him that she was going to self-publish it.

He advised her that his company was first a book publisher, and he invited her to send him what she had. "He told me to send him four chapters, the table of contents, my media kit, and he would let me know what he thought of my little book," said Melinda.

She did. Six weeks later, Peter called to say that he liked what she had written, and asked her if she had any more chapters and if she could write a mini book proposal. She had no idea what a book proposal was, but she was sure that someone in her network would know.

Stay engaged and in Touch with Your Network

A friend recommended Paul B. Brown, who, unbeknowst to Melinda at the time, was a contributor to the *New York Times* and the author of the highly acclaimed book *Customers for Life*. Melinda called him and advised him of the situation, and he agreed to help. She sent the proposal, along with three more chapters to Peter, which he loved. The publishing board unanimously approved the proposal and she got a book deal. She also added people to her network and created relationships that would mutually add value for years to come.

Every Kick Can Be a Boost

Melinda's book was due to the publisher just as the financial markets crashed in 2008. After turning in her manuscript, she received the crushing news that they were postponing the release of the book until March 2010—a whole 18 months! Because of the crash, their thought was that no one would be thinking about starting a small business. Needless to say, Melinda was devastated by this news, as she had already started winding down her business, thinking she was about to start a national book tour. Now, she was back at zero—again. She recalled that Bill Gates once said if he had two dollars left in the world, he would spend one dollar on PR. And that is exactly what she did. She hired a publicist who happened to be savvy with social media. When Melinda told her publicist about the publisher's decision to postpone the book for 18 months, to her surprise the publicist thought this was great news and replied, "Great. We have 18 months to build your author platform, and I know just what to do."

They went to sign up on Twitter using her name as her handle, but to her surprise, @MelindaEmerson was already taken. "You mean there's another Melinda Emerson?" she thought. Unfazed, her publicist encouraged her not to panic and to think of a nickname. As a professional, Melinda was not really happy about this. She had never been referred to by a nickname and did not think her name would translate to a catchy nickname. Her publicist told her to focus on a name that told people who she was and what she did. They continued to brainstorm, and after several attempts, they finally settled on SmallBizLady. Immediately, Melinda thought that it fit and was something she could work with. The SmallBizLady brand was born.

Be Consistent and Deliberate When Posting to Social Media

Over the next 18 months, she started working Twitter like a full-time job—posting daily to Twitter, sharing information with colleagues and industry peers, answering small business questions, blogging content from the book, and sharing personal stories from her adventures as a new mother. People really responded to her postings, and each week she gained more followers while building anticipation for the book release.

Once the book came out, she had built a substantial enough audience that she was able to secure modest speaking engagements, which really helped to grow her brand.

Be More Interested Than Interesting

By the time the book had come out, she had developed a significant following on Twitter and started fielding questions about business challenges from small businesses around the country. She became highly sought after for her advice and insights, and began to notice some significant trends when she was responding to people. She saw this as an opportunity to create a weekly Twitter chat for small business owners called #Smallbizchat, the hashtag she uses to convene her audience live on the Internet every Wednesday at 8–9 p.m. ET. It has since grown to become the largest and longest running weekly chat on Twitter, reaching over 3 million followers each week.

By this time, corporations were using Twitter as a part of their social media strategy. They also started taking notice of Melinda's followers and the content she was providing. In January 2011, she received a call from Pitney Bowes, who wanted her to help them implement a social media strategy to reach small businesses. Soon after, other Fortune 500 companies followed. To Melinda's surprise, within 20 months of getting on Twitter, she had enough of a following that she was able to monetize her platform with corporate consulting work, and becoming a brand ambassador with corporations targeting the small business market.

Pay Attention to Industry Trends. Know What's Now, But Focus on What's Next.

Seeing the changes that were occurring, Melinda quickly changed the name of Quintessence Multimedia to Quintessence Group and reengineered it as a marketing consulting firm, working with Fortune 500 companies to build marketing campaigns to engage small business customers. After about a year, several media outlets began reaching out to Melinda to contribute to media publications including Entrepreneur.com and the *New York Times*. These were paying gigs that further helped elevate her brand.

Throughout her career, her network had been instrumental in many of her achievements. She was an early adopter of social media and used it to create a community, extending her network online and offline. Her strategy of developing and sharing compelling content to demonstrate her expertise became the secret sauce for her business and its reinvention. She credits her networking skills with allowing her to build the business of her dreams.

50 Billion Dollar Boss Moves
Managing and cultivating relationships can be challenging. To create a network to help grow your net worth, you should:

- Strive to build relationships that are more than just transactional;
- Stay engaged and in touch with your network;
- Understand that every kick can be a boost;
- Be consistent and deliberate when using social media;
- Be more interested than interesting;
- Pay attention to industry trends, and know what is now but focus on what is next.

CHAPTER 7

Where Is the Money? Solutions to Fund Your Business and Business Development

Twyla Garrett, President and CEO, IME, Inc.

It is no exaggeration that everyone felt the effects of the economic crisis of 2008. Unfortunately, no other community was impacted more than the African American community. In an analysis of Small Business Administration's data by the *Wall Street Journal*, African Americans were badly hit by the recession, particularly in real estate and foreclosures. As a result, African Americans, as compared to other ethnic groups, reported a lower net worth, lower credit scores, fewer assets, and negative equity on property, making them less attractive to lenders. The subsequent long, hard road to recovery touted a renewed emphasis on small business in order to rev up the economy, but has resulted in tighter credit, stricter lending criteria, and cutbacks by banks, which in many ways hampered the growth it was supposed to spur.

The report further states, U.S. financial institutions made $382.5 million in Small Business Administration loans to black-owned businesses in the fiscal year ended Sept. 30, 2013, representing just 1.7 percent of the $23.09 billion in total Small Business Administration Loans. This percentage is down sharply from 8.2 percent of overall Small Business Administration loan volume in fiscal 2008. By number of loans, black-owned small businesses got 2.3 percent of the federal agency's roughly 54,000 loans in 2013, down from 11 percent in 2008, the start of the financial crisis.

The growth of African American women-owned businesses over the past two decades is especially remarkable given that African American women often partially underwrite their enterprises with their own funds. A 2010 survey of members of the National Association of Women Business Owners showed that:

- 63 percent of female respondents used credit cards to finance their businesses;

- 44 percent used private sources, such as personal savings, family, and friends;
- 37 percent used a business line of credit;
- 13 percent used a commercial or bank loan;
- 11 percent used a personal bank loan;
- 4 percent used a loan guaranteed by the SBA; and
- 2 percent used equity capital.

Although business capital has become more accessible to entrepreneurs through targeted capital-access programs such as microenterprise and venture capital funds, African American women face extra challenges in obtaining this capital. Almost half of all African American women business owners say that they have faced obstacles when trying to obtain financing. Research has confirmed that women are more likely to be turned down for loans or receive loans with less favorable terms than their male counterparts. Additionally, a review of studies on small businesses revealed that minority-owned businesses, when compared with similar white-owned businesses, face greater difficulties in accessing loans from financial institutions, including having their loan applications rejected more often, receiving smaller loans, and experiencing higher borrowing costs. In 2011, only 11 percent of capital-investment funds went to women entrepreneurs, while 89 percent of capital investment went to male entrepreneurs, despite the fact that 20 percent of top entrepreneurs were women.

Especially when it comes to accessing capital to start and grow a firm and increase its performance, women, and African American women in particular, face difficult challenges. The response has been to show even more determination to reach their goals.

Twyla Garrett is an extraordinary serial entrepreneur, corporate speaker, and author. She is the Founder, President, and CEO of several enterprises, including Investment Management Enterprises, Inc.

(IME), which specializes in program management, business process engineering, system integration, customization, web-enablement of legacy applications, enterprise-scale database design and development, solution-focused web/software development, and IT and ERP consulting and staffing services for the federal government; Garrett Entertainment Co. (GEC), a restaurant and real estate development company whose projects include the development of a $1.5 million entertainment complex in Cleveland, Ohio; and T&R Transportation (Ft. Washington, Maryland), a provider of reliable, regional, interregional, and nationwide less than truck-load (LTL) and truck load (TL) service to customers large and small. Her firm employs over 50 people, has offices in Richmond, San Diego, and Washington, DC, and does business all over the world. In 2012, she was personally invited to speak at the White House on the issues of creating jobs, economic growth, and the controversial fiscal cliff. She shares her compelling story of how she overcame immense personal challenges to start several business ventures and earn a reputation for self-funding most of her business deals.

A Rough Upbringing Is an Understatement

Twyla grew up in the inner city of Cleveland, Ohio. "To say that my upbringing was rough would be an understatement," recalls Twyla. She is a survivor of emotional, physical, and sexual abuse who sought to climb her way out of despair, family trauma, and financial disadvantages. Twyla never misses an opportunity to speak about this, as she truly feels that it helped to shape her business philosophy and fuels her relentless drive for success. Further, it has provided the foundation for many of her ventures, as she always tries to incorporate an opportunity to help someone else who might need a second chance. She has been praised and recognized in many of her ventures for helping and employing homeless or formerly incarcerated people and providing at-risk teens with jobs and an opportunity to learn business skills.

An Epiphany

Twyla attended Ursuline College, which she credits as really clarifying her vision of the possibilities for her and her own capabilities. "Everything came together for me at Ursuline College," says Twyla. "It is where I got my business insight and my discipline. The dedication and the mentoring I received at Ursuline made a significant difference in my life." While attending Ursuline, Twyla was a detail-oriented, mathematically gifted accounting student. After graduation, she signed on with the Defense Finance and Accounting Service in downtown Cleveland. She eventually moved to Washington, DC, and served a stint with the Joint Chiefs of Staff at the Department of Defense. She stayed there for nine years as a foreign military sales program manager. In that capacity, she found herself selling used planes and ships to nations that could not afford new ones.

While it never bothered her, Twyla was the only African American and woman in the department. However, as time went by she saw that colleagues who happened to be white males were getting promoted, while she was not. She began to realize she did not have a future with this department. It was at this moment that she set her plan in motion to leave the organization and start her own business. Twyla realized her background gave her experience and a unique skill set that not many people of color had. In 2000, she started Investment Management Enterprises, Inc. (IME), and set a goal to leave her Department of Defense job within the next few years. Her company carved out a niche specializing in homeland security, disaster preparedness, cyber security, and business process engineering.

Today, Twyla is one of the leading and most respected homeland security, disaster preparedness, and cyber security experts in the country.

Turning Pennies into Dollars

As a young, single, successful woman who was making a good salary working for the federal government, Twyla was able to afford a comfortable lifestyle and enjoy the rewards of her hard work. When she decided she was ready to make the transition to entrepreneur, she knew all of this would change. As a new business venture in a nontraditional business—and, as Twyla suspected, as an African American woman—she knew that it would be difficult for her to get funding for her business. Undeterred, she set out to fund her business the way that made the most sense to her: she would fund it herself. Always thrifty, she pared down her expenses and began saving her money. Although, her business was service based, she would still incur start-up costs. Further, as a contractor, she might not receive payment for 30, 60, or 90 days after services had been rendered. Twyla knew that this would severely impact her cash flows and that she needed to be prepared if it was a while before receivables came in. When she had saved about $50,000 in start-up funding, she set her sights on doing business with local municipalities. "During the day I was a government employee. At night and pretty much any free minute I had, it was all about IME, researching, and responding to proposals, scheduling meetings and trying to make connections" recalls Twyla. She quickly bid on and won small contracts, honing her ability to prepare winning proposals and developing a strong track record with clients. Any profits that she made, she reinvested back into the business.

By 2003, Twyla decided it was time to quit her job and focus on her business full time. Within three years after she started her company, she was doing quite a bit of work for local governments and became aware of a federal bid opportunity that she knew that she would be able to perform. She was ready to grow her business to include federal contracting, but due to conflict of interest issues, she could not do this if she was still a federal employee. She quit her job and prepared and submitted her bid. To her surprise, she did not win. Understandably, Twyla was disappointed and now, unemployed. Although she had worked for the federal government for years and understood the process, she realized that the transition from employee to contractor with the federal government was very complex and multifaceted. She had to make her new company a success. Further, bidding on federal contracts was very different from bidding on contracts for local municipalities. It required her to develop a different strategy. She set out to develop partnerships with larger firms and sought to find a mentor to help her make the necessary connections and gain experience as a federal contractor. As the firms that she partnered with would win projects, she gained more exposure and experience, and soon found that her firm was being sought out and asked to respond to bids.

After nearly 15 years in business, Twyla's success as a contractor for the federal and local governments has created yet another opportunity for her, and she has affectionately become known as "The Fed Biz Lady." This term was coined by one of her clients after seeing all of the encompassing services her company had grown to provide and the success that she achieved as a contractor. "I'm always willing to help people understand the complex bidding system used to contract work with federal, local and state governments," says Twyla. "I'm hopeful I can make the process easier to understand for new and established companies." She launched a new business in which she plans to provide one-on-one services, webinars, and easy-to-follow white papers on the subject of working with the federal government. She thinks that the more small businesses can contract with the federal government, the better. Jobs can be created right here at home, and the marketplace will be more competitive, saving Americans significant amounts of money down the road.

The Making of a Mogul

Although she knew that she wanted to be an entrepreneur since she was 16, Twyla asserts that she did not set out to become a mogul. She says that growing up in a challenging city neighborhood, her only goal "was not to be poor." With the success of IME, Twyla began to explore and pursue other entrepreneurial ventures in her hometown of Cleveland. The idea for her first expansion came when she had decided to buy two luxury penthouses in an up-and-coming entertainment area in Cleveland known as The Flats. As she looked around, she saw the promise of the space next door to the residential building where she had just purchased her penthouses. She approached the developer, Stonebridge, about what would become her most ambitious entrepreneurial venture yet—a mixed-use entertainment complex to include a restaurant, coffee bar, and market. Inspired by her many trips to Italy, she envisioned an open-air experience, offering patrons the opportunity to sip lattes in the lounge, browse in the artisan market, have dinner, and dance the night away to live music.

Stonebridge loved the idea and thought it was a perfect fit for the area. They became partners, with Twyla investing $1.5 million of her own funds in the project. "This experience was great because it allowed me to explore my creative side, which I do not always get to do with government contracting. Making a significant investment in the project also made a difference as I was not just a 'silent partner' and was able to have a say in the direction and vision for the project," she adds. Twyla was actively involved in all aspects of the project, which was credited with pumping new life into the area. To ensure she preserved the authentic European feel she envisioned, she had a crew of Italian cinema set designers flown in to transform a major portion of the former factory building into an indoor version of an Italian piazza that included Tuscan walls, cobblestone Roman streets, and nine-foot replicas of Venetian party masks. Although

Twyla later sold her interest the project, it became the model for future development projects that she hopes to replicate in other markets, including Washington, DC. One of her proudest accomplishments with the project was that it was seen as a place that offered support to area artists and, as Twyla says, "people who need a second chance."

Create a Plan Outlining Your Long-Term Goals and Objectives to Determine Right Financing Options

Like most entrepreneurs, Twyla always knew that she wanted to have her own business, but she just was not sure what she would be doing. Her years of working with the federal government allowed her to see the opportunities that existed for her skill set and strengths. Once she figured out how she could service the government, it became easy to prepare to go into business for herself.

"IME was my first business and I love it," she says, "but it has allowed me to pursue so many other passions and entrepreneurial interests from restaurants to real estate development. I can come to the table with my own funding, which helps to get a lot of things done. People take notice when you are bringing both ideas *and* capital." She sets aside a portion of her revenues to invest in potential opportunities. "In this business, I consider this one of the costs of doing business. I never want to miss an opportunity or a partnership because I did not have the funding to invest in it," she says.

When it comes to planning for the future, Twyla says her company is always reviewing their portfolio and assessing the business in yearly intervals (typically, one, three, and five years), both by category and logistically. "This holistic approach to looking at the business allows me the ability to determine what our needs will be and the best financing options available to help us achieve our goals. Also, we've just reached a point where it's not always advantageous for us to fully fund," she explains.

By reviewing the business at annual intervals, they can best determine their growth strategy and how they will achieve that growth. Presently, her companies are planning for the next five years and trying to strategize whether to grow organically or through acquisition. Not afraid of making ambitious plans, Twyla wants to grow IME into a $100 million enterprise. She is also looking at potential acquisition targets in the range of $5 million to $10 million.

Throughout the years, IME's homeland security expertise customers have included the US Department of State, the Federal Emergency Management Agency (FEMA), and the Department of Defense. One of her goals is to broaden the company's federal presence. Twyla says she is presently pursuing a 25 million dollar contract with the Transportation Security Administration (TSA). She is also looking to expand into the private sector with an eye toward the health-care industry and opportunities to offer cyber security and IT support services to corporate clients. She predicts that within three to five years her private sector sales could go from zero to exceeding her federal government business.

She also looks at her business logistically to determine the best market(s) for her to expand in, in order to better serve her clients. She recently selected Atlanta, Georgia, as her new corporate base because office rents are a third of what they are in Washington, DC. The location also provides her with close access to potential large customers including Delta Air Lines and AT&T. Due to the magnitude and scope of the project, she has been courted by venture capital consultants. She is looking to raise 1.5 million dollars to establish her new corporate headquarters, a comprehensive campus that she expects to be office space, a showroom, and a research facility. Although she has the capital in place to fund the expansion herself, she has determined it might be best to keep cash in reserves and take advantage of the relatively low cost of money. She sees this as an opportunity to establish a relationship with venture firms on a relatively small investment with an eye toward further investment opportunities.

Focus on Maximizing Sales Rather Than Incurring Debt

When Twyla decided to start her business, she did not have the luxury of turning to family and friends for start-up capital. She knew that being an African American woman in a high-risk, nontraditional business might make it difficult to obtain outside capital. So Twyla made the decision to keep her job and save her money while she grew her business. She significantly cut her personal expenses, leaving her with capital to invest in the business and enabling her to focus on winning contracts. It was only after a few years, and after she had won a sizable number of contracts that she finally made the decision to leave her day job and focus on the business full time.

Another reason Twyla opted to save to fund her business is that, as a contractor you do not always win every project for which you submit a bid. Further, if your firm is the successful bidder, there could be a significant amount of time between when the work is performed and when your firm actually receives payment. It is important to have sufficient cash flow to keep the business afloat during this time without having the worry of paying back costly loans.

Today, Twyla is frequently courted by banks offering her business everything from loans to substantial lines of credit. Although she is now able to get financing for anything that she needs, she remains selective and strategic when she seeks outside funding. "It took some time to get to this point. Just like in business, I am very selective about who I partner with, even in a banking relationship," says Twyla. She credits this strategy of not incurring debt to grow her business with allowing her to be nimble and strategic in going after contracts that she knew that she could successfully perform, while also establishing relationships that benefited her in the long term.

Consider Alternative Funding Options

Twyla started her business before the days of crowd funding, IPOs, and *Shark Tank*. Depending on the type of business, crowd funding has created an opportunity for businesses to generate a large amount of funding in a relatively short amount of time, without the typical requirements of collateral and with fewer restrictions on use, payback, or any of the other terms required by traditional lending institutions. Twyla went the old-school route and just saved money and reinvested as she made money. She felt this was the best option for her. "There are definite advantages to using your own money to fund a business," she says. "However, in this time of tight credit restrictions there are numerous low-risk alternatives that provide businesses with the cash flow that they need to grow their business. I'm not sure if my business model would have been different if I had received funding from other sources, but as a small business advocate, it is good to know that these options are now available for people." After 15 years in business, only recently has she begun to embrace venture funding for her latest business expansion.

Consider Collaboration to Achieve Your Goals
(a Percentage of Something Is Better Than
100 Percent of Nothing)

Twyla credits the success of her company to her strategy to collaborate with other firms that had more experience with federal contracting. She had the benefit of being mentored, which allowed her business to gain invaluable experience and proficiency. Today, she frequently collaborates with other firms on opportunities, which has allowed her to expand the breadth of her company's expertise in a number of areas. She has also become a highly sought-after partner for projects across the country. As a speaker at various events, she frequently extols the virtues of developing collaborative relationships—particularly for women-owned businesses—that can lead to business success.

50 Billion Dollar Boss Moves

To determine the best solutions to fund your business and boost your business development efforts, you should:

- Create a plan outlining your long-term goals and objectives to determine the right financing option;
- Focus on maximizing sales rather than incurring debt;
- Consider alternative funding options; and
- Consider collaboration to achieve your goals (a percentage of something is better than 100% of nothing).

CHAPTER 8

Making You a Priority: Leveraging Internal Strengths

Ricki Fairley, Founder, President, and Thought Leader of Dove Marketing

When starting and running a business, there is always a to-do list. Most entrepreneurs will tell you they would not have it any other way. While we are all accustomed to multitasking, sometimes making our own well-being a priority becomes the last item or gets pushed to the next day. Many entrepreneurs neglect their most important asset—themselves. Unfortunately, it often takes something catastrophic in order for us to prioritize ourselves and our health.

Ricki Fairley is the Founder, President, and Thought Leader of Dove Marketing, an agency with a mission to deliver iconic thinking, strategic problem solving, and creative genius to clients seeking profitable business results. She is a seasoned marketer with over 30 years of marketing experience, including 20 years in brand management at Johnson & Johnson, Nabisco, Reckitt & Colman, and the Coca-Cola Company, and over ten years in agency leadership, encompassing strategic planning and consulting for several Fortune 500 companies. Ricki has received numerous awards and accolades, including the Leadership Award from the Creative Thinking Association of America; the Association of National Advertisers Multicultural Excellence Award for African American advertising for the Obama for America campaign; the Game Changer Award from *Café Mocha*; and the *Atlanta Tribune* and the US Commerce & Trade Research Institute Excellence in Marketing Award.

She has been named a Top 100 Marketer by *Black Enterprise* magazine and has been inducted into the HistoryMakers. Her client roster includes the American Association of Retired Persons (AARP), Dr. Julianne Malveaux, The Hester Group (USDA, USMBDA, Corner Bakery Cafe), Added Value, The Howard Theatre Restoration, and TV One.

Prior to starting her company, Ricki held the position of chief marketing officer and partner at IMAGES USA, a boutique advertising agency in Atlanta where she managed strategy and planning for all IMAGES USA clients and led the implementation of successful and award-winning campaigns for Amtrak, Sara Lee, Wachovia, Wells Fargo, Glory Foods, the National Black Arts Festival, Teach for America, and Brown Forman. She also directed the agency's new business development initiatives that maintained its position as a leading multicultural marketing firm.

Ricki holds a BA from Dartmouth College and an MBA from Kellogg School of Management at Northwestern University. She is the president emeritus of the Black Alumni of Dartmouth Association, and board chair of Kenny Leon's True Colors Theatre Company. She serves on the board of directors for R&B singer Ne-Yo's Compound Foundation. Ricki manages the relationship between the Links, Inc. and the White House Office of Public Engagement as a member of the National Women's Issues and Economic Empowerment Committee, and is a member of the Silver Spring, Maryland, Chapter of the Links, Inc.

She is a member of the board of trustees for the Triple Negative Breast Cancer Foundation and works diligently to garner publicity for breast cancer awareness. She is also a member of the 2011 class of Leadership Atlanta.

Ricki shares her story of how a life-changing diagnosis forced her to reprioritize her life, which included starting a business and putting herself at the top of her personal to-do list.

Destined for Success

Ricki went to college at Dartmouth College, where she earned her BA degree in English. As a highly sought-after Ivy League graduate, she was able to consider a number of programs. A counselor at Dartmouth told her she should check out Northwestern University's business school. At the time, although the school was the number one school in the country for brand management, it was not yet the world-renowned Kellogg Graduate School of Management that we know it to be today (it was renamed Kellogg during Ricki's second year). They were gaining a reputation as a top-tier marketing program.

She took a marketing class and fell in love with it, noting that all or most of her professors were authors of marketing textbooks that, even today, are used all over the world. Back then, brand management was a new format that more and more consumer products companies were adopting as a means of managing their marketing efforts in a more strategic and entrepreneurial manner. Although both her parents were educators, she recalls having her professors explain to her father exactly what brand management was, what she would be doing with her life, and assuring him that she would have a great career ahead of her.

In those days, companies held nightly receptions and actively recruited black students for scholarships. She received a full scholarship for graduate school from Quaker Oats. While searching for an internship closer to her home in Washington, D.C., a friend had just gotten an internship with McNeil, the makers of Tylenol. So Ricki applied and earned a spot as well. Upon graduation from business school, she received a full-time offer of employment from McNeil.

Corporate Star

When Ricki arrived at McNeil in 1982, she was suddenly plunged into the tragic Tylenol tampering case, which claimed the lives of seven people. She recalls that the episode was extremely terrifying and beyond anything she could have ever imagined. For several weeks, it was all boots on the ground, all the time. It was with that experience that Ricki cut her teeth in corporate marketing. She stayed at McNeil for a few years after that and sought opportunities in other categories. If you check your house, chances are there is a product that Ricki has worked on as a brand manager. After leaving McNeil, she went on to work at companies such as Johnson & Johnson, Nabisco (Life Savers, Bubble Yum), and Reckitt & Colman (Lysol, Easy-Off, Black Flag, Mr. Bubble) to name a few.

Although she did not set out to become an entrepreneur, Ricki was increasingly challenged with assuming entrepreneurial functions within the corporate environments in which she worked. At Reckitt & Colman, trade marketing was becoming an area of focus, with major accounts asking for special pricing and promotional considerations. In response to this, she was asked to start a trade marketing department, allocating marketing budgets by trade accounts (i.e., Sam's Club or K-Mart), or by channel (i.e., food, drug, mass, warehouse club), and managing spending based on their sales.

She was later recruited to Coca-Cola to re-engineer their marketing services department, which was renamed MarketingWorks and functioned like an intercompany agency. Her group serviced all 21 of the company's brands and was responsible for the activation of all promotions that the company had in the market. She estimates that her group could easily be working on a thousand promotions at any given time. She grew her division from 50 employees to 150, and had annual staffing and marketing budgets of $10 million and $400 million, respectively.

Ricki loved what she did and felt like she had her "dream job." However, she hit the glass ceiling (which was no surprise—she had hit it two times in previous stints). At the time, she was the third-highest-ranking African American woman at Coke and the only one with profit and loss responsibility, in that her actions directly impacted the bottom line for the company. She was in a visible position and had a very important role within the company, but in the big picture of Coca-Cola USA, she did not feel respected. As an African American woman, she realized there were probably not a lot of options that would be available to her or that she would be interested in, and began contemplating her next move. She was sure that she did not want to go through the process of giving everything she had to another company, knowing eventually there would only be so far that she could advance within its ranks.

Ricki left Coke and became a partner at IMAGES USA. She managed the strategy and planning side of the business, while her partners handled the business development. This was an ideal arrangement, and ownership was just what she needed at this stage of her life. It gave her the freedom to do what she loved, with the opportunity to share in the profits derived from her efforts.

However, all of her elite training and accomplishments could not have prepared her for what was to be her next life-changing experience.

Deadly Diagnosis

The day started like any other high-stress day in the life of a type-A working mom and wife. During her annual gynecological checkup, her doctor found a lump in Ricki's left breast. But all Ricki could think about was she had to get back to work, figure out what she was going to cook for dinner, and make plans for her upcoming week-long business trip. "I didn't really have time for the mammogram, sonogram, biopsy, or that diagnosis," she recalls. But soon enough, after a positive biopsy and a confirmed breast cancer diagnosis, she had to make time and deal with it. The pathology report confirmed that she had triple-negative breast cancer. What was supposed to be a tiny, early-stage tumor turned out to be fast growing, aggressive, and malignant.

"You Have to Figure Out How to Remove All Stress from Your Life"

In Ricki's first meeting with Nancy, her nurse and breast cancer coach, Nancy started the conversation with, "When you walk out of here today, you have to figure out how to remove all of the stress in your life." Of course, Ricki denied having stress in her life. She had grown so accustomed to being a multitasking, miracle-working African American woman, she never had time to entertain the concept of stress in her life. Nurse/coach Nancy then added the bomb-dropping statement that would change her mind-set and dictate her behavior throughout her healing process and, really, for the rest of her life. "Your life depends on it." Hearing these words, Ricki surmised that her life as she knew it would never be the same again. However, as she began to reflect, that might not be such a bad thing.

Develop a Survivor Mentality

Ricki had to make decisions about her physical and emotional state in order to remove the stress. She took the most radical medical route available—a double mastectomy, aggressive chemotherapy, and radiation. Her mastectomy identified that the cancer had spread to her lymph nodes, putting her at Stage 3A. Stage 4 is terminal. While many members of the medical community consider this an extreme measure, Ricki felt it was the best choice for her and a choice that her doctors were proud of her for making. She credits Dr. Yvette Williams, an assistant professor at Emory University's School of Medicine and a cancer survivor who also underwent the procedure. "She was a mentor and dear sista-friend and really helped me to make this decision and undergo this process," says Ricki. It was also during this time that she tapped into her inner strength to make hard decisions to change her life.

Incorporate Activities That Bring You Joy and Fulfillment

While she was undergoing chemotherapy to defeat the physical cancer, Ricki had to start working on the *emotional* cancers in her life.

In short, she had to reprioritize all aspects of her life, and she had to come first. She filed for divorce from her husband of 30 years. She also changed her environment. After her divorce was final, she sold her house in the suburbs of Atlanta. An avid lover of the water, she moved to the beach.

She then made the decision to sever her relationship with her business partner. While this was a necessary decision, it was also one of hardest, as she needed income more than ever. She was undergoing expensive treatments, had a daughter in college, and needed to support herself.

She went to the annual Black Enterprise Women of Power Conference, which she attended every year. This conference is for African American women corporate executives. After a particularly tense call with her former business partner to discuss the terms of her exit, Ricki decided that she would start her own agency. She proceeded to brainstorm names for her company with her girlfriends. She decided on Dove Marketing as she felt it represented her survival, healing, and—for the first time in a long while—the freedom and liberation she felt. She focused her energy on building a client roster, specializing in firms that have a favorable impact on society. Her first client was the Obama for America campaign. She found that writing and producing all of the radio ads targeting African Americans for President Barack Obama's re-election became a part of her healing process. Several other clients soon followed, making the launch of her business a huge success and the right decision for her. "Although I transitioned, and in some ways, downsized my life, I have never been happier or more fulfilled," says Ricki. "I've always felt the work that I did was important, but in many ways, I've found a renewed serenity, contentment, and purpose that I might not have explored had I not received my diagnosis," she adds.

She also began to volunteer for causes and with organizations that resonated with her, such as Kenny Leon's True Colors Theatre

Company and R&B singer Ne-Yo's Compound Foundation, which works to enhance the well-being of youth growing up in foster care and group homes. She also began volunteering for the Triple Negative Breast Cancer Foundation, where she works diligently to garner publicity for breast cancer awareness.

Develop a Supportive Network

Through her year of recovery and healing, and also in her professional life, Ricki says she was blessed with love and caring from her family and so many friends from every area of her life. The six weeks of initial healing time after her mastectomy were really hard.

"When I woke up from the surgery, I felt like a truck had hit me and then backed up over me again," she recalls. "It was no joke: I had chemo on Fridays and was pretty much out of commission until the following Wednesday. One thing I am grateful for, though, is the fact that I was never alone. I could not have made it without my incredible mom, my force-to-be-reckoned-with younger sister, my two beautiful, brave, brilliant, and bodacious daughters (who were 19 and 26 at the time), and my supportive and loving sista-friends who stepped in and stepped up, taking care of me and pouring unconditional love on me while I healed."

Put Your Oxygen Mask On First

Being a frequent traveler for work, Ricki recalled the words that the flight attendant says just before the plane takes off: "Put the oxygen mask on yourself first, before helping others." She had to learn to make herself a priority in every aspect of her life. "Some of the hardest decisions I ever had to make were made while I was going through chemo," she says. "After everything that I've dealt with, I know that I have the strength to overcome anything." She considers herself not just a breast cancer survivor but a survivor in life.

50 Billion Dollar Boss Moves

Starting and running a business requires you to be healthy. To make yourself a priority during this time, you should:

- Develop a survivor mentality;
- Incorporate into your life activities that bring you joy and fulfillment;
- Develop a supportive network; and
- Put *your* oxygen mask on first.

CHAPTER 9

Keeping It Moving: Developing a Resilient Mind-Set

Lola C. West, Managing Director, WestFuller Advisors, LLC

When you start and run a business, the stakes can be very high, and your very livelihood can depend on the success of your enterprise. Some entrepreneurs have a romantic notion of entrepreneurship, in that they are in love with the idea of saying they have a business, but do not necessarily have the passion for the business needed to ensure its success, especially when the 'ish gets hard. They realize that making the decision to start a business is easy, but running a business is harder than it looks.

There are many articles that explore the "entrepreneurial mind-set" and the attitude and skill sets that are needed to successfully run and maintain a business. With the average life span of a business being around five years, one trait that seems to be the greatest attribute and remains consistent for all entrepreneurs is developing a resilient mind-set to help carry you through the tough times. Lola shares her dynamic story of how she used each experience to "rebrand" herself and transition from one career to the next.

High Expectations

Lola C. West grew up in a West Indian family. There was never a question about whether she would go to college, be a professional, or earn a very good salary. "The level of expectation for you to always do your best was a given in my family,"recalls Lola. "When I was in the fourth grade, I came home from school excited to share my math test score of 97 percent. My mother looked at it and asked, "Why didn't you get 100 percent?," adds Lola.

The next week, she got 100 percent. She ran home to share the good news with her mother, only to be told, "That's the mark you should get." No big congratulations—just that a perfect score was the expectation. This rearing set the stage for her self-awareness, direction, and work ethic. Change comes easily when you give yourself permission. As a youngster, you do what your parents expect. As an adult, change is then easier.

As a child, Lola had aspirations to be a doctor. After all, she was named after one. But once she was in college, that goal changed. In 1965, Lola enrolled at Brooklyn College. The college was 98 percent white. For Lola, chemistry and biology proved to be very difficult. There was a remedial course scheduled at 7:00 a.m. for students who needed help. Unfortunately, the only people who showed up for the course were the smartest people in the class, so it turned into a "remedial" class for the brightest students.

Racism was alive and well, and Lola got no support from the department for her needs. She changed majors. After toughing it out for four years, she decided to become a lawyer, and upon graduation from Brooklyn College was accepted to New York University School of Law. She could not get any financial aid, and her parents, although middle class, would not or could not afford the Ivy League tuition. So Lola fell back on Plan B (always have a Plan B!), and accepted a $16,000 scholarship to get a master's degree in Urban Planning at Hunter College.

Upon receiving her master's from Hunter, Lola took a job with a consulting firm where she evaluated the Federal Elementary and Secondary Education Act (ESEA). As a consultant, the pay was $150 a day, which in those days was substantial. She then worked for less than a year as the executive director of a Head Start program in Manhattan, and then as a counselor for John Jay College. These three positions took her through a very difficult economic time of double-digit unemployment and inflation. This made her keenly aware of the tentativeness of the job market and how the economy worked.

Early Lessons

When Lola was 18 years old, she read that a successful person makes about $1,000 annually for each year of one's life. She thought that was a very good marker, and that was what she decided to do. So imagine her surprise when at the age of 35 she was making $45,000, and she discovered that this amount was not going to give her the life she had envisioned for herself. To that end, Lola began to understand why owning a business and being in charge of her destiny was a route she would eventually seek.

In 1977, Lola accepted a job as a building administrator for a facility at Willowbrook Developmental Center run by United Cerebral Palsy Associations of New York State, Inc. (UCPA, NYS, Inc,). This was the infamous facility on which Geraldo Rivera produced an exposé on the neglect of patients, a piece that catapulted him to fame and won a Peabody Award. During that time, Federal Judge John Bartels ordered the state to take several steps, including reducing the population at the facility. Judge Bartels awarded seven buildings to UCPA, NYS, Inc., who was chosen to run the seven buildings at Willowbrook because of the exemplary work it had been doing at The Nina Eaton Center, also located on Staten Island. As an administrator for UCPA of NYS at Willowbrook, Lola quickly rose through the ranks, and within two years had become the unit-wide administrator for all seven buildings in the complex. She now managed 2,300 employees and a budget of approximately $22 million. She went on to open other facilities in the community for mentally retarded and dual-diagnosed clients. Her tenure with UCPA, NYS, Inc. was commemorated when she received a proclamation proclaiming February 13, 1987, as "Lola C. West Day" in New York City.

Soon after receiving this honor, Lola was hit with a realization. After working for the agency for 11 years, she had hit the glass ceiling. While she was the highest-ranking African American executive at the agency, a white colleague who had not received nearly the accolades and successes that she had, and whom she had trained, was promoted over her.

She decided her time there had come to an end and talked to her mother about her plans to resign.

With her upbringing, willfully quitting a well-paying job (she was making $58,000 at the time) was unheard of. As she expected, when Lola told her mother that she was thinking about resigning from UCPA, NYS, Inc. she was incredulous. After all of these years, Lola can still recall their conversation:

"How can you leave that good-paying job?" asked her mother.

"I'm not happy there!" replied Lola.

Her mother responded, "What does *happiness* have to do with *work*?"

A Generational Shift

Lola saw her mother's reaction as a generational shift in the meaning of the Protestant work ethic. Unlike her parents, her intention in her work was to be happy, fulfilled, empowered, passionate about what she was doing and, hopefully, able to do good things in the process. She had no interest in just "working." At that moment, Lola was determined to do what made her happy and gave her fulfillment.

She resigned from her job and never looked back.

She felt a little vindication when, in 1988, a year after her resignation from UCPA, NYS, Inc, her accomplishments were again acknowledged with her inclusion in the sixteenth edition of *Who's Who of American Women*.

Don't Be Afraid to Try New Things

Lola had frequently explored her own gifts through doing exercises in the career book *What Color Is Your Parachute?* by Richard Bolles. Lola found that her best strength was in entertaining and taking care of other people. The book suggested that she was an effective party planner, so she opted for that as a career and looked to do events for people. She had been planning parties since the seventh grade and had orchestrated a number of dinner parties with her mother. One of the first consulting jobs she was hired to do after leaving UCPA, NYS, Inc. included organizing and producing special events for the Board of Education of the City of New York. Her first big event was organizing a "Farewell-Thank You" party for outgoing Mayor Ed Koch and Deputy Mayor Stanley Brezenoff, hosted by Richard Wagner, president of the NYC Board of Education. What started out as a three-day-a-week consultant job turned into Lola's new business!

Lola became the owner and president of Dean Sayles Enterprises, Inc. (DSE). DSE was an event-producing, fundraising, and audience development business, and was the first black-owned licensed professional fundraising company in New York State. Her clients included The College Fund/UNCF, NAACP, The Studio Museum in Harlem, National Urban League, The African American Institute, The Boys Choir of Harlem, and the (Charles B.) Rangel for Congress Committee '96. Between 1993 and 1995, Lola worked for August Wilson and Camille Cosby on audience development, bringing hundreds of black theatergoers to Broadway via traditional black organizations. She organized numerous national conferences, and in 1993 she coordinated events and fundraising efforts for the former South African president and world-class humanitarian Nelson Mandela. She warmly recalls an excerpt of the letter she received from Mandiba (his Xhosa clan name): "Your thoughtful planning and competence in the execution of the event as well as your commitment to our common cause must be the real infrastructure upon which the larger and successful event rested. I want to personally congratulate and thank you, Lola, for all your efforts."

In 1996, Lola was the event producer of Jessye Norman Sings for the Healing of AIDS. The event won the Forty-Second Annual Emmy Award for Outstanding Societal Concerns Programming.

Focus Time and Energies on Situations You Can Control

After ten years in the business, Lola saw a shift in the industry. She realized that she would no longer be as successful as a fundraiser because the optimization of the computer was pushing major corporations to centralize their giving through foundations. As a professional fundraiser, one of the ways money is raised is through selling tickets to individuals or groups to an event that an organization is hosting, usually a gala, dinner, or reception, etc. Where she was previously able to get several tables out of a mega corporation, she was now only able to get one table. She had focused time and energy on her vocation and had seen the pitfalls. "I knew that a significant decrease in how much I was able to raise would not bode well for my clients or my reputation. You can blame market conditions for only so long," recalls Lola. She dissolved her company and took three years off to think about what she was going to do.

During her three-year hiatus from job hunting, she dabbled in the stock market. In a conversation with a dear friend who was also a headhunter, Lola lamented that she still had not found her next career. Her friend remarked she should do what she loved. Like many women, Lola was not really sure what that was, but her friend pointed out that she appeared to love financial planning and the stock market. Lola realized that during the years she had not been working, the stock market had become an educational course for her. She immediately called a friend who was a senior executive at a major brokerage house and asked what she thought about her becoming a financial advisor. Her friend thought it was a good idea.

Lola soon got an interview for the position of financial advisor.

Walking through the doors of a Fortune 100 company was a completely new experience and proved to be a challenge. As an African American woman in a white man's world, the racism was palpable.

When Lola arrived for her job interview, it was obvious that the white female interviewer was not expecting to see someone of color.

It was also evident that the interviewer had forgotten about their appointment. She took Lola to lunch in the company's cafeteria, along with a wholesaler with whom she was also scheduled to meet. The wholesaler seemed uncomfortable and left within 20 minutes. The interview continued and they got to the salary portion. The interviewer indicated the base salary for the position was $24,000, to which Lola thought, "Really?" All new financial advisors are paid a base salary until their training/licenses are in place and they are issued a producer number. Salaries are then based on annuitized/commissioned business. She asked if the salary were negotiable, and the woman replied that it was. Lola could barely remember the last time she had made so little money. "At 52, I felt this number was not just insulting, it was downright depressing," recalls Lola.

Lola did not receive an offer. "I was definitely disappointed but undeterred," recalls Lola. She was advised by another African American senior executive to ask the interviewer to release her name back into the candidate pool so that she could still be considered when other positions became available. She was unaware that she could even do this, but asked the interviewer to release her name. Lola's original contact at the company put her in touch with one of only two African American directors who hired her over the phone, with a salary that she felt was appropriate until she built her book of business. Lola knew with the contacts that she had, she could make this work. Having worked her way through the door, she began her new career as a financial adviser.

It was 2001 when she embarked on her new career at the broker-age house. As a fifth-generation New Yorker, Lola had always lived and worked in the city. She now had to work in the New Jersey office because that was the only office that had an African American director in her area. To get an idea of the racism she endured during that time, out of more than 100 retail offices in the United States, only two had black directors—one man, one woman. Lola went to the brokerage house with what she considered a "golden Rolodex," having raised money for Nelson Mandela; organized an event for Jessye Norman that was attended by a host of celebrities including Whoopi Goldberg, Elton John, Anna Deavere Smith, Maya Angelou, Toni Morrison, Max Roach, Bill T. Jones, and others; and having spent years raising funds for major charitable organizations.

The exams for the licenses required for the job were difficult and challenging, but she persevered. She soon learned that as a financial advisor at any major company, or house, as they are commonly referred to, you own your own business. They do not provide you with clients. You are responsible for bringing in your clients. Essentially, you are running your own business under the brand of a major house. Lola found this autonomy exciting and exhilarating.

Her next challenge came with the building of a team. Team building in the financial services industry is seen as the most advantageous way to build a book of business—that is, you partner with others to create a team that works together to provide various services to its clients. The problem was that no white team wanted to partner equitably with African Americans. While her colleagues found her to be a great resource to introduce them to her roster of celebrity clients, they did not view her as an equal partner in business.

With the future in mind, she recruited a younger man, Ian Fuller, to join her team. She befriended him and watched him for two years. She saw that he had a strong work ethic. He was always at work when she got there in the morning and was still there when she left in the evening. She then began to informally mentor him, helping him with assets to complete the training program and develop his skills as a broker. She eventually invited him to join her team, which he accepted.

Before the emergence of diversity and inclusion programs and training during her tenure, the brokerage house proved difficult at best. It was discriminatory, racist, and sexist. When the company began to stumble in the market, another financial institution stepped in and acquired it. The racist atmosphere went from bad to impossible. Many senior-ranking African Americans systematically resigned, but in actuality, they were terminated, demoted, or their positions eliminated. As with most organizations with very little diversity, the African American employees were a tight-knit group. Over the years, the small cadre of African American senior managers and colleagues had become valued mentors and advisors to Lola, and she attributes their mentorships as one of the keys to her success at the company.

One of the reasons Lola had wanted to work at this particular company was that it was at the top of the food chain and had the most robust training program. Once the brokerage house was acquired by the larger financial institution, Lola felt the merged company lacked integrity in its business practices and how it treated it employees, which she found unacceptable. One of the things she prided herself on was her refusal to compromise her integrity.

As more of her colleagues of color were being forced out, Lola saw the handwriting on the wall. Lola was one of the few who lasted for almost ten years. Unfortunately, as had happened in the past, it became time to move on.

Welcome Adversity as a Test for Growth

Going to another brokerage house was not on Lola's mind. Although times had changed since she first started in the industry, the adversity she had experienced at the previous brokerage house made it impossible for her to conceive going through that experience again. While the administrative challenges, racism, and fees at the brokerage house were frustrating and often demoralizing, the negative experience, as often happens, served as an extraordinary growth and learning experience at many levels. Throughout all of her experiences, Lola never lost sight of her desire to have her own business. Thus, the next step for her was clear: it was time to start her own company.

Lola and her partner, Ian Fuller, became founding partners of WestFuller Advisors, LLC, which specializes in the wealth management needs of, and provides strategic insights, financial planning, and investment advice to, high-net-worth clients, multigenerational families, entrepreneurs, executives, business owners, and nonprofit institutions in both the United States and abroad.

Lola recalls, "Having trained and worked at one of the top brokerage houses in the country for nearly ten years, and surviving the rigors of one of the toughest working environments one could ever imagine experiencing, one would think that fear, of any kind, would subside, but it does not!"

Lola had several reasons to be nervous. Leaving a well-known brokerage house to start a smaller, boutique brokerage business during a recession was a risky proposition. The first years out of the brokerage house were no cakewalk. "My salary was severely impacted but I knew that was temporary as I have always been employable," says Lola. Further, when dealing with people's money, calming the client's fear and concern about the trustworthiness of the broker are paramount and take time to build. "This probably concerned me even more than the lack of salary. I no longer had the cover of a large company. I was asking people to entrust their savings and, in a sense, their futures, with me. I never want to take that lightly or for granted," adds Lola.

According to the SBA, over 50 percent of small businesses fail within the first five years. For the financial services industry, the rate of failure is much higher, with 58 percent of these businesses failing in the first four to five years. For Lola, having her business successfully reach and pass the five-year mark was a tremendous accomplishment. "Although the fear of having your own business never really goes away, I finally felt that the business was on the path to long-term success," she says. Her fifth year was also when the company experienced one of its best years.

Stay Committed to Goals and Objectives

Lola is a firm believer that her faith in God is what has allowed her to create a sustainable career, develop a resilient mind-set, and keep things moving. The journey has been arduous but joyful, and has provided her with an assurance that keeps her continually pressing forward. WestFuller Advisors is thriving, and Lola has realized her lifelong dream of being of service and changing lives by providing a bespoke, boutique financial services company. As a boutique agency, relationships are a crucial component to their success, and they have been able to create a client roster that allows them to specialize in niche clients. Lola recalls, "One of the very first pieces of art work that I bought was by the African American abstract expressionist Norman Lewis. A client of mine knew that I had a piece of his work and introduced me to Lewis's daughter—who happens to be my partner Ian's mother!" Because of this relationship, they have been able to cultivate a roster of some of the top artists in America.

Ever the planner, Lola says she strategically chose a partner much younger because she is stuck on legacy. Her partnership with Ian ensures her legacy with WestFuller Advisors will continue.

50 Billion Dollar Boss Moves

Change in business is inevitable. To keep things moving and develop a resilient mind-set, you should:

- Focus time and energy on situations you can control;
- Not be afraid to try new things;
- Welcome adversity as a test for growth; and
- Stay committed to goals and objectives.

CHAPTER 10

Faster, Smarter, Harder: Taking Your Business to the Next Level

Dr. Michele Hoskins, Founder and CEO, Michele Foods

Whether the long-range plan is to keep the business and bring children into it, or sell it to a large corporation, growing the business is at the forefront of every entrepreneur's mind. Making the decision to move to bigger and better things brings both huge rewards and tremendous risks. How to grow the business raises a slew of questions: Do you grow the business organically through increased sales or do you acquire or merge with another company? When is the right time? Have you exhausted capacity at your present state? Are you ready to handle the growth? Do you have the money and resources to grow? Like most things, deciding to grow the business is not a one-size-fits-all proposition. Determining the right strategy for your business is a process and requires a plan.

Based in Chicago, Illinois, Michele Hoskins is the founder and owner of Michele Foods, Inc., which produces Michele's Honey Crème Syrup, Michele's Butter Pecan Syrup, and Michele's Maple Crème Syrup. She has been featured on the *Oprah Winfrey Show* numerous times and in other major media outlets including CNN, Fox News, *People* magazine, *Fortune*, and Black Entertainment Television (BET). She has received numerous awards and recognitions including the 2002 "Entrepreneur of the Year" award by the Women's Foodservices Forum, the Top 100 Professional Women by *Dollars & Sense* magazine, Emerging Company of the Year by *Black Enterprise* magazine, the Entrepreneurial Women Award in 1998, and the Madam Walker Entrepreneurial Award. She also received an honorary doctorate from Johnson & Wales University.

She tells her story of how she took a family recipe for syrup and turned it into a sweet, multimillion-dollar company.

Humble Beginnings

During the late 1970s and early 1980s, Michele and her husband separated, leaving her to raise their three young daughters. She soon realized that she would not be able to pay the mortgage and feed her children on her current income. As she was edging closer to hitting rock bottom, it occurred to her that it was time to get more mileage out of her great-great-grandmother's legacy—a secret family recipe for syrup, formulated for the plantation family that she cooked for. Michele had no idea whatsoever how she was going to do it, but with blind ignorance, hopes, and prayers, she set out to make this dream a reality.

Coming from a family of cooks, Michele was the only daughter and had cooked quite a bit growing up. Her mother had a recipe that had been handed down in her family from her great-great-grandmother, America Washington. The recipe was for pancake syrup that they called honey crème. Family tradition held that the third daughter in each generation would get to have the recipe, and it would remain a secret to everyone else. Michele's mother was the third daughter, and thus she ended up with the recipe. Although Michele was not the third daughter, she was the *only* daughter, and was very curious about the recipe. She finally persuaded her mother to let her "hold" the recipe for her own third daughter, Keisha, and began practicing making it for her family. Michele finally got the syrup to the point where family members could not tell the difference between her and her mother's syrup.

After reading an article that said women would rise during the 1980s, Michele resolved to become an entrepreneur. It was at that moment that she decided to start Michele Foods, Inc., and her product would be Michele's Honey Crème Syrup. She reasoned she could hand her daughters a business rather than just a recipe, and that would be a much better legacy.

The Early Years in Business

During the time she was starting her business, Michele overcame many challenges, including getting into her first stores, being accepted and taken seriously as an African American business-woman, dealing with product shelf life, experiencing personal illness, and being on welfare. Eventually, Michele's company secured distribution in Jewel and Dominick's, a major Midwest grocery retailer. After nine years as a regional product, the company could pay its bills and sustain itself. She was interacting with customers at as many local events as she could possibly attend, handing out samples everywhere she went. She was doing in-store product demonstrations (think Sam's Club samples during the weekend) with her daughters, where they made countless pancakes and served them with Michele's Honey Crème Syrup.

The problem was that she was serving people stacks of delicious pancakes, but she was not make any *money* that would stick around!

Lessons in Growing a Business

Some open doors are nothing but a setup for failure. The federal government in Washington was talking about equal opportunity for women and small businesses. Michele had been able to leverage being an African American businesswoman, as diversity and affirmative action were hot topics. When she started talking to corporations, she realized she was great for the diversity checklist, but after they gave her the opportunity, it was up to her to determine how she was going to make money. She began thinking how hard she was working every day, sacrificing for her family, yet she was going home without a paycheck. It took everything that she had just to keep product on the shelves, pay a copacker to make and bottle the syrup, and pay the bottle and label suppliers, the transportation company, and everybody else. She realized that she did not have enough profits to hire anybody, buy a car, or buy a home. She had achieved what she wanted, but she felt stuck.

Ask for Help

One day while meeting with a colleague, Michele struck up a conversation about her dilemma. She explained she was not making any money, just recirculating it. She finally asked, "How do you make money in this business? How do Aunt Jemima and the others make money?"

He told her that the big competitors sold in volume all over the country. He went on to explain that she needed more orders. While the comments seemed simple and obvious, for Michele, this revelation was like someone had switched the lights back on after a storm. From this conversation, Michele had her marching orders but she was cautious. "This revelation forced me to approach my business in a totally different way. I was nervous but also exhilarated about the new direction I was about to take my company," says Michele.

Step Out of Your Comfort Zone

Michele's caution with taking this new direction was warranted, having experienced several instances where she nearly lost everything while building her business. "When I first started my business, I was working for Fashion Fair cosmetics, a brand manufactured by Johnson Products Company, the venerable African American company and publisher of *EBONY* and *Jet* magazines. I was leading a double life—working at Fashion Fair during the day and moonlighting to get the syrup to market at night," she recalls. Her copacker was getting the syrup ready for retail when Michele quickly realized she was going to need much more than the $25,000 she had borrowed from her brother in order to get the product to market. It seemed every time she went into the copacker's office, they needed more money. "They would say, 'Okay, Michele, we've formulated the syrup. We need $16,000 to go to the next step' or 'Bring your daughter and your mom to take pictures for marketing materials, but it's going to cost you $2,300 to do the photos and then you've got to get them printed,'" she recalls. She determined, at this rate, she would need $150,000 to continue to the point where the syrup would be a marketable product. Having no one to turn to, she realized she had to raise capital herself and began selling her possessions. So every time the copacker needed money, she would find something to sell. She eventually sold her condo and she and her three daughters moved into her mother's attic.

Another obstacle came as Michele was readying her product for market. She was becoming less focused on her day job at Fashion Fair and knew she could not last there much longer. She had been very successful at Fashion Fair and was asked by Mr. John Johnson, the eponymous entrepreneur and founder of Johnson Products Company, to start teaching skin care at beauty colleges. She respectfully declined the opportunity and proceeded to tell him she had started her own company. He was not happy about this revelation and, although she was making his company lots of money, she was fired. Her job was her sole source of income—to provide for her family and to fund her business. This was all that she had. She was in debt and could not borrow any more money. After getting fired, she knew that she did not have a lot of people to turn to for help. She needed money and quickly! She also needed a place to raise her family, as she knew she could not stay in her mom's attic for much longer. As an entrepreneur, she was not eligible for housing aid, and in order to get help that she needed, she decided to apply for welfare. "I went from being an entrepreneur with this great recipe, envisioning myself being on the road to millions, to the reality of being a mom with three kids on welfare," recalls Michele. She eventually got housing but it was hardly adequate. "Sometimes we were so short on resources, that I gave syrup to the landlord in order to pay my rent," she says. She was on welfare for nine months, and the lean times felt longer than that. However bleak the situation seemed, though, Michele never lost sight of her bigger picture. She still perceived herself as the entrepreneur on the way to greatness and her situation as nothing more than a means to an end. "This simply became a way for me to take care of my kids while I continued to build something for our future," she says.

She recalls another time when she learned the hard way the importance of shelf life. She received an urgent call from her copacker that the product was not stable and would become rancid after 60 days. She knew this could be the death of a product and could get you immediately pulled from the shelves of stores. She worked feverishly to find another copacker, and after a long exhaustive search, she found Joe Laforge. He owned a copacking manufacturing company called Kalva Corporation, which was located in another town. When she met him, she explained her situation. To her surprise, his response was, "I know what product you're talking about. You're talking about a honey syrup. I saw it on the shelf and I know your problem." He told her what he would use to stabilize her product—butter buds. This was butter that had the fat and water removed and was then made into a powder. He said that would solve her problem while still retaining the "butter flavor," recalls Michele. Now that she was assured he could produce the syrup to her specifications, Michele switched copackers.

Having had these experiences, Michele was cautiously optimistic about her plans to grow her company. As she began ramping up her plans to move her company in the new direction, she realized she needed to learn the business through and through in her own backyard before making another move. She had settled into a comfort zone and had spent all her time in the Midwest because she knew the region. She could go to see her product anytime she wanted, whether it was driving to the West Side of Chicago to see it on shelves or going to stores on the North Side. She had friends and family keeping an eye out on product in their neighborhoods. If something was wrong—if it had been pushed to the back of the shelf, for instance—they would fix it, and she liked the comfort or having an informal cheering section. She felt validated after years of sacrifice and hard work, and had finally gotten a handle on things enough to prove that she was not crazy to start a business with the family syrup recipe. Still, it was time to break out of the Midwest cocoon, and she hardly knew where to start.

Take Advantage of Unexpected Events

Michele adopted what would become her Monday morning ritual. For a year and a half, every Monday, at around 10:30 a.m., she called Flagstar, the parent company of Denny's Restaurants. Even though they resisted her from day one, she wanted to do business with them. Every time she called, they gave her the runaround. It was very frustrating, but she was determined, and all she knew how to do was ask to be considered at the very least.

One day she opened the newspaper and read that Denny's was in hot water with a racial discrimination case against them. It was yet another horrendous episode in which an American corporation had denied basic humanity to African Americans. Among other things, the suit alleged that blacks were being asked to prepay for their meals. She knew this might be her window of opportunity. She had been calling the company for a year and a half, and now that they were involved in this high-profile mess, they would need someone like her. She knew that it probably would not be about the syrup but about the relationship, positive publicity, and photo opportunities. But she would not let that deter her, and she approached Denny's like she did every other customer that she contacted. She knew that her product was good and that this was an opportunity for everyone to win: they would get a relationship with an African American businesswoman, and their customers would get the great syrup they deserved. She aggressively pursued Denny's, and the day came when they decided to give her a shot. The Denny's deal gave Michele entrée into the foodservice industry, which was very different from the grocery retail model that she was used to. Yet, it presented another facet of opportunity for Michele's company. She just had to figure out how to make it work.

With the Denny's deal, Michele figured out a way to generate $300,000 in revenue without owning a plant, or making or transporting the syrup. She hired a copacker to produce the syrup, which she resold to Denny's. She would make about $1.00 on every case. This was a business-to-business model that did not require her to fret over labeling, advertising, marketing, PR, or any of the other things she had to do with her other accounts. Foodservice became a significant part of her business, and in 1997, she joined the Women's Foodservice Forum. In 2002, she received the first annual Entrepreneur of the Year Award, which recognized a woman owner, founder, or franchisee of a foodservice operation who had successfully grown her business, developed other women leaders and given back to the foodservice industry.

Michele was also able to leverage all of the advertising and publicity she received through her relationship with Denny's. At the time, Denny needed positive press on the heels of the discrimination lawsuits and settlements. They featured her in a print campaign and invited her to speak at industry events about her experience working with them. Their PR department made sure to talk about their relationship with her, and as a result, she started to get national press placement. She was featured in *Fortune* magazine and the *Wall Street Journal*. In the interviews, they always wanted to know how she did it. She made sure to talk about the fact that it was her great-great-grandmother's recipe. "The legacy became the focus more than the syrup. Nationally, it became a human interest story," Michele recalls.

Leverage Your Media Exposure

While still working to grow the retail business, Michele was doing in-store demonstrations and events all over Chicago. A local television producer saw her at one of these events and saw the crowds of people that were always gathered at her demonstration. One station interviewed her, then another. The attention she received from the local media always helped to increase sales. She was accepting invitations to speak about her business and the syrup on small radio stations, and the black press was writing feature stories about her. She began to realize the magic of media exposure and how it related directly to sales. One day, Michele got a call from WGN-Channel 9 News to do a segment with her family about the syrup. She thought it would be like any other interview, but little did she know this interview would change her business forever. Reporter Steve Saunders came to her home with a camera crew. Before they arrived, Michele and her family had been up for hours preparing a feast of fried chicken and waffles and a variety of other foods that went well with Michele's Honey Crème Syrup.

After the segment aired, Michele got her first real taste of the power of television for a small company like hers. Someone from Walmart saw the segment and called WGN inquiring about her. They spoke with Steve, the reporter who had done the story. Steve called and told her that Walmart was interested in talking with her further about possibly coming into their stores. This was it! She knew they would be her ticket out of the Midwest. When Michele spoke with the people at Walmart, they told her about a couple of programs that they had in place that could get her syrup onto their shelves. At the time, Walmart was an aggressively growing retail chain. They had very diverse customers coming through their doors looking to buy various products. The company recognized that all of its customers were not just white folks. With all the talk of diversity, Walmart was not taking this lightly.

A man named Wayne Easterling was the manager of Walmart's Minority and Women-Owned Businesses Development Section. His job was to go out and find companies like hers, companies with viable products so that he could groom them as Walmart suppliers. At the time, Walmart had a program called "Made In America," which supported domestically made products. To get a product into Walmart, it had to be produced in America, which meant assembled by American labor with raw materials produced within the United States. Walmart sent her applications for both programs. She qualified for both programs as she was 100 percent minority owned, and everything she bought was American produced—corn syrup from ConAgra in Nebraska, butter from a supplier in Wisconsin, honey from farms in Michigan, and the rest of the raw materials produced domestically as well.

Walmart put Michele's syrup on shelves in selected stores. This was the first step in attaining her goal of expanding out of her comfort zone.

Don't Be Afraid or Intimidated to Attract and Pursue "Big Investors"

With the entrée to Walmart, the need for a business plan and for more capital to grow became even more pronounced. Michele got some books and took a stab at a rough plan, which showed that she really could use the help of someone who knew a great deal more about these things. But she pressed on and kept trying to fine-tune her plan until she could work out something else.

Her minister introduced her to a Chicago-area businessman who was looking for an investment opportunity. This was the break that she had been looking for, but pitching to stores to put her products on the shelf was very different from pitching to someone to invest in the business. She continued to work on her business plan in preparation for her meeting. She finally got the call for the meeting from the potential investor and his financial advisors. The investor decided that he liked the potential of the company, and his banker agreed that this would be a good venture for him.

He agreed to invest $150,000, but he would not provide it all at once. It was set up as a line of credit to use as she needed money to cover expenses for such things as bottles and caps, labels, and raw materials. Through this arrangement, he would simply write a check to cover these costs. Michele would then submit a budget to him every month stating how much she had spent, and he would take care of it.

She kept a meticulous log to track what she borrowed from the investor, and was careful not to abuse this resource. She knew that it was a limited arrangement. It was meant as a steppingstone to a day when she could comfortably cover her own business expenses, and that she had to pay it back.

It was a wonderful relief to have this support. Another great aspect of the deal was that she could move into the investor's office space in LaGrange, Illinois, which gave Michele's company the added resource of professional facilities from which to work. Up to this point, Michele Foods had been a home-based business. She filed paperwork with the investor regarding the terms of repaying the borrowed monies and signed the document, confident that she would soon be in a comfortable position to begin paying him back and to move into her own office space. Michele saw this opportunity as the boost she needed to move her company from a "mom-and-pop" operation to the scale and capacity that she envisioned!

Now that she had this investor, she was able to devote her time to servicing and growing the foodservice side of her business and the Denny's account. The Denny's account allowed her to have consistent and adequate cash flow. She relied on the money from Denny's because as a growing company, she did not have a lot of accounts, just Jewels, Dominick's, and Walmart. She was not moving a lot of products in those stores, and thus the inflows from Denny's were keeping her afloat. She started approaching other large companies, including General Mills and Ahold USA, the parent company to Stop & Shop. She was able to branch out into chains such as Bi-Lo and Safeway. She also landed a relationship with Church's Chicken. And she was able to expand her product offerings as well, and introduced two new products—Maple Honey Crème and Butter Pecan syrups.

Michele recalls, "I knew I had finally made it when in 1999, I got the call from Oprah. I had just gotten the Denny's contract and we were growing distribution in several stores. I was getting regular publicity, which was really helping to push the product through to consumers. Oprah had a segment called 'the millionaire minute' and her producers wanted to feature me." Every time she went on Oprah, she saw her sales surge. "If we were in 90 Walmarts, we would see a surge in all of those stores. We were not saturated all over the country but we were able to maximize our appearance to the hilt wherever we were. It was a great boost. I don't think we would have grown as fast as we did, had we not appeared on Oprah," she adds. She went on to appear on Oprah three times.

Today, the company's products can be found in more than 10,000 food stores nationwide including Stop & Shop, Super Walmart, Albertsons, Kroger, Publix, Super Target, Cub Foods, H.E. Butt Grocery, Jewel Foods, Safeway, and Dominick's Fine Foods.

50 Billion Dollar Boss Moves

Growing your business is a process and will not happen overnight. You should:

- Realize some open doors are a setup for failure;
- Ask for help,
- Step out of your comfort zone;
- Take advantage of unexpected events;
- Leverage your media exposure; and
- Not be afraid or intimidated to attract and pursue big investors.

CHAPTER 11

Coding for the Future: New Frontiers for African American Women in Technology

Laura Weidman-Powers, Cofounder and CEO, CODE2040

In Silicon Valley, diversity in the digital technology industry—or more precisely, the lack thereof—has been a topic of discussion. Increasingly, companies have been challenged to increase the diversity in their ranks. There have been numerous reports and initiatives designed to get minorities and women interested in STEM careers—science, technology, engineering and mathematics. It is no secret that these jobs are among the fastest growing and yield the highest wages. According to the National Math and Science Initiative, STEM job creation over the next ten years will outpace non-STEM jobs significantly, growing 17 percent as compared to 9.8 percent for non-STEM positions.

It has, in fact, become a skill imperative. In an op-ed piece in the *New York Times* entitled "A Future Segregated by Science?" (February 2, 2015), Charles M. Blow hit the mark by stating, "The United States needs to attract and retain more talent and diversity in science, technology, engineering and math (STEM) to keep America competitive. Pursuing opportunities in STEM-related fields becomes even more critical for minorities and women in that it provides access to overcoming entrenched economic inequality by race and gender."

Laura Weidman-Powers is the Cofounder and CEO of CODE2040, a nonprofit that creates pathways to success in the innovation economy for blacks and Latino/as. Laura is a 2013 Echoing Green Fellow and a 2013 Stanford Social Innovation Fellow. In 2013, *The Root* named her one of the 100 Most Influential African Americans, and Goldman Sachs named her one of the 100 Most Intriguing Entrepreneurs. Her work has been covered by the *New York Times, Forbes,* NBC, Bloomberg, *Fast Company*, NPR, *USA Today,* and others. She shares her story of how her background in nonprofits and her own experiences in technology led her to become cofounder of one of the most culturally relevant nonprofits in technology, a trusted adviser to leading technology companies, and a foremost voice on diversifying the technology industry.

Not Your Typical "Techie"

Laura Weidman Powers is not what you typically think of when you think of the technology industry or Silicon Valley. She is from the East Coast and admits to having an "East Coast mentality." She earned a BA cum laude from Harvard College, where she majored in psychology and co-ran an organization called CityStep that greatly influenced her interest in public service. The group helps middle school students build self-esteem through an arts curriculum that fosters community involvement and creative self-expression. Upon graduating, she fully intended to secure a job at a nonprofit. However, she ended up receiving two fellowships to support her work starting a branch of CityStep in West Philadelphia. The program is still in place today, which is something Laura takes pride in. "It was an extraordinarily powerful experience," she recalls, "and even more so knowing I laid the foundation for an influential organization."

Going Back to Cali

After leaving CityStep, Laura kept her work in education going, cofounding with Harvard classmates a for-profit tutoring company with offices in New York and Los Angeles. She was also increasingly becoming interested in the tech world. It was an industry that she had not really considered before and one in which she did not have a lot of experience. Her first job in tech was as a project manager in a small web development shop in New York. After a while, she was soon ready for a change. Intrigued by the carefree, nontraditional mentality of the West Coast, she headed west to attend Stanford

University. She obtained her MBA/JD with the intention of returning to a career in the nonprofit sector. Instead, she decided to take an opportunity with a consumer web start-up based in Los Angeles, where she served as vice president of product design, redesigning the product development process to be inclusive of engineers.

Laura was looking for her next opportunity when she met former Stanford classmate Tristan Walker, for coffee. Tristan is a Silicon Valley veteran of organizations including Foursquare, Andreessen Horowitz, and most recently, CEO of Walker & Co. Brands. He and Laura were in the same section in a class of 375 students at Stanford. They worked together on a number of case studies, projects, and presentations and, coincidentally, they both spent one summer in Los Angeles, interning with different companies. As friends, they kept in touch when they graduated and got together whenever she was in town. During coffee, the conversation ventured toward diversity in Silicon Valley. It became clear that both of them wanted to do something to address the inequities and inequality among people of color in the area. In typical Silicon Valley fashion, Tristan pitched an idea he had been thinking about and proceeded to try to convince her to be the point person for the project. Despite having started up a branch of CityStep and a tutoring company, Laura had never seen herself as an entrepreneur. However, being in Silicon Valley for the first time, she felt a sense of huge potential and was captivated by the energy that was all around her. At the same time, she noticed there was not the same level of diversity that she had been used to growing up in New York or working in West Philly.

Immediately, she saw the potential of the project. "I thought about what I was excited and passionate about and capable of, and thought, hey, this is something I can do." She also thought about her own experiences since moving to Silicon Valley. "I was going to meetups and industry events, realizing there weren't a lot of people that looked like me. This lack of diversity, and seeing the power of the tech sector, was a big part of the inspiration for CODE2040." At just 29 years old, Laura was the perfect person to lead a cultural shift such as this. She had built up a resume stuffed with accomplishments: degrees from Harvard and Stanford and a background in entrepreneurship, nonprofit management, youth development, and technology. It was an opportunity to combine her love of nonprofits with her interest in technology. This was the opportunity she was destined for. The program that they brainstormed about was pretty straightforward, but she soon found that building a company was very different from building a program.

A New Paradigm

They named the organization CODE2040, because, as Laura explains, "Our country is undergoing a massive demographic shift. Census projections show that by the year 2040, people of color will be the majority in the United States. It is important to have that shift reflected in the ranks and the leadership of innovation hubs like Silicon Valley. Currently, studies show this is far from the case with fewer than one in eighteen technical employees in the Valley being black or Latino/a. CODE2040 aims to open doors for underrepresented minority talent in the Valley in order to help diversify leadership in the Valley and in the US as a whole in the area of high-tech innovation and entrepreneurship."

With Laura as cofounder and CEO, and Tristan as chairman of the board, CODE2040 was created to fix two problems they saw contributing to the lack of diversity in Silicon Valley: 1) lack of awareness as there is not adequate knowledge about the opportunities in Silicon Valley and how great it can be to build a career in the innovation economy, and 2) lack of access because we hear stories about companies going public or being acquired or securing tens of millions of dollars in venture funding. The truth is, most of the high-performing people of color do not have access to the networks that one needs to be incredibly successful in Silicon Valley.

The organization boasts an impressive board of heavyweights that reads like a who's who in technology and entrepreneurship, including Ben Horowitz—author, technology entrepreneur, and cofounder and general partner of the venture capital firm Andreessen Horowitz.

Admittedly, companies in Silicon Valley have a long way to go when it comes to diversifying their ranks and providing opportunities to people of color. However, top companies are now stepping up to make the industry more accessible. Intel, which pledged $300 million to increase the diversity of its US workforce the year 2020, represents the largest investment yet in diversity by a technology company. "We were tackling this when the focus was not what you see in the media today," recalls Laura. "When we started going out to talk to companies, rather than having the sole focus be on diversity for diversity's sake, we really thought about the message that we thought companies would like to hear. We knew that everyone is always looking for talent, so that's what we focused on, rather than just the diversity message. It just happened that our talent came from diverse and underrepresented backgrounds. Initially, companies were skeptical, as they were used to only looking at talent from top-tier or Ivy league schools," she says. "It took us a while to change their perceptions. We found that many firms wanted to do something, they just didn't know how to go about it," she adds.

In just three short years since the organization began, the industry has shifted, and they have more companies that want to work with them than they have the capacity to include. In fact, there is a waiting list of companies interested in working with them. Over the years, they have had partnerships with several of the top technology companies in the world. Their flagship Fellows Program has grown from 5 students to a projected 40 students in summer 2015. It has graduated nearly 50 fellows, many of whom have gone to work for companies such as Facebook, LinkedIn, and Uber, and 90 percent of Fellows received return offers from their summer employers. Over 1,000 students have applied to become CODE2040 Fellows, and over 200 companies have expressed interest in hosting Fellows for summer internships. Laura and Tristan hope to expand the Fellows Program and eventually work with companies year round.

Look at Entrepreneurial Opportunities That Can Support the Technology Industry

Early in her career, Laura had the benefit of exploring several professions until she found her niche. While she did not set out to start a business nor did she create a traditional technology firm, her organization supports the industry by providing them access to a network of highly qualified interns and, ultimately, employees, ensuring their company's future success and hers.

Every Meeting Is a Chance to Build Your Network

As with any industry, the importance of a strong network cannot be underestimated. As Laura recollects, "when I arrived in the area, I did not have a strong professional network and I saw few people that looked like me." Ironically, she was able to create and build a business that not only helps companies make crucial connections to diverse employees but also ensures a strong network and sustainable pipeline for future generations so that they are not discouraged by the lack of diversity. "Although the industry is making progress to diversify, change takes time and it can be very isolating when you don't see people that look like you," she says.

Networking has been another way that she has continued to build her network and grow the company. "In this industry, networking is engrained in the culture and is seen as a natural extension of the work day. I always try to say yes, because that is where you are likely to make your next deal, meet your next client, or court a potential investor. We once met a prospective investor and made a follow-up appointment to make a presentation for him. He ended up not investing in the company, but he did offer us free office space in New York City whenever we were in the area," she says. "Had we not met him at an event, we might have missed this opportunity," she adds.

Consider Opportunities to Develop New Skills Sets and Experience in Technology

Although the prospect of going back to school sounds daunting, many universities, organizations, and companies have become more proactive and responsive by offering workshops or extended learning courses that allow participants to develop new skill sets and learn how to sell to new customers. These are usually available at a much lower cost than a traditional college stint and are offered at times that accommodate a busy schedule, such as evenings, weekends, and distance learning. Sometimes a career refresh is necessary in order to stay relevant.

Sometimes You Have to Go against the Status Quo

Earlier this year, CODE2040 received backing from Google for a new pilot program for minority technology entrepreneurs in three cities. Starting in Chicago, Austin, and Durham, North Carolina, they will give minority entrepreneurs in each city a one-year stipend and free office space while they build their start-ups. The three CODE2040 entrepreneurs-in-residence will become catalysts for minority technology entrepreneurship in those communities. "Silicon Valley is the epicenter of the tech world and is the headquarters of some of the world's most powerful tech companies. Working on diversity issues in Silicon Valley means going against the status quo. We are trying to change the ratio of employees at large companies, bring inclusive techniques to established hiring practices, and infiltrate relatively closed, powerful networks. Spreading to small tech hubs presents a huge opportunity for us to impact inclusion in tech across the country. Our focus is on changing what might or could be, and our work in Silicon Valley can influence that and set an example for the rest of the tech world. We've found that in the smaller tech ecosystems around the country, often the cultures and norms around talent and inclusion are not yet set. We have the opportunity to help these places incorporate inclusion into their DNA from the ground up," Laura explains. "It's an opportunity to create cultures where the divide has not become entrenched like it has in Silicon Valley," she adds.

When asked about their exit plan, their goal is to execute themselves out of existence. "By the year 2040," says Laura, "we hope we'll have worked ourselves out of a job and CODE2040 isn't needed anymore."

50 Billion Dollar Boss Moves

Technology is presenting unprecedented opportunities for minorities and women. To take advantage of opportunities, you should:

- Not be afraid to consider opportunities in nontraditional fields;
- Consider the technological prospects in your industry;
- Realize that every meeting is a chance to build your network;
- Consider opportunities to develop new skills sets and experience in technology; and
- Sometimes go against the status quo.

CHAPTER 12

Why Should Guys Have All the Fun? Entrepreneurial Opportunities in Nontraditional Industries

Joy Rohadfox, President and CEO,
Rohadfox Construction Control Services Corporation

The construction industry is one of the last traditionally male bastions. However, women are increasingly joining this industry and getting involved on the entrepreneurial side of the business. The US Census Bureau counted 152,871 women-owned construction firms in 1997. By 2007, that number had jumped by 76% percent to 268,809. If women in corporate America have a glass ceiling, women in construction have a concrete ceiling.

For the past 15 years, the Initiative for a Competitive Inner City (ICIC) has compiled its Inner City 100 list, highlighting the fastest-growing urban small businesses in America. In 2013, the list included 28 women-owned construction businesses, a doubling in percentage since it began tracking urban small business growth in 1999.

According to a recent article by *Fortune* magazine, this growth is a direct result of a 35-year-old goal set by the Office for Federal Contract Compliance Programs. Since 1978, federal contractors are required to employ women for 6.9 percent of the total construction work hours on any federal project.

Joy Rohadfox is President and CEO of Rohadfox Construction Control Services Corporation (RCCSC), an engineering and construction management firm, based in Atlanta, Georgia. They are considered to be one of the oldest minority construction and program management firms in the United States, catering to water/wastewater facilities, aviation, rail and transit systems, roads and highways, and the federal government. She is the key driver for RCCSC's strategic direction, and being a very young woman in a male-dominated field, she knew that, in addition to the expected challenges facing a female minority owner, she would also have to live up to the values and business principles that her father, Ronald Rohadfox, former CEO, instilled in her and in the company.

She shares her story of how, despite having little or no previous industry experience, she was able to assume the reins of a second-generation business, while the economy and the firm were on the brink of a collapse and rebuild it into one of the most respected and venerable minority- and woman-owned construction services firms in the country.

Is There a Doctor or a Lawyer in The House?

Joy was born in Durham, North Carolina, and grew up in Hillsborough. She went to the University of North Carolina at Chapel Hill and majored in Public Health, with plans to go to medical school to become a pediatrician. Determined to "get out of North Carolina," she moved to Atlanta to further her postbaccalaureate studies. After earning her graduate degree from Georgia State University, she was eager to continue to advance her professional life, and prepared for the LSAT and was accepted into law school. All of these plans changed, however, when she received word that her father was in a terrible car accident.

Building a Legacy

Joy's father, Ronald Rohadfox, started the company in 1976. Like many entrepreneurs during that time, he wanted to take advantage of business development programs that were creating opportunities for minority-owned businesses. As the face of the company, everything about the business fell on his shoulders. At the height of the company, they grossed revenues of $20 million, and had 200 employees and offices around the world. "We did work all over the country, and a lot of the work we won was not just because of our capabilities, but because of the strategic relationships my father had built over his many years," says Joy. Her father was always on the road and was known to have meetings in three different cities in one day.

Outside of working there during the summer, usually in an administrative capacity, Joy never had much involvement in the business, nor had she considered an entrepreneurial career for herself. A self-proclaimed "education fanatic," Joy enjoyed being in school. But when she received news of her father's accident, she decided to hold off on law school. "I figured I could always go back to school, but continuing my father's legacy was more important to me," she says.

A New Face for an Old Company

As her family was adjusting to her father's rehabilitation from his accident, he suffered several other health setbacks, including a triple bypass and a knee replacement, rendering it almost certain that he would never return to his company. Shortly after, one of the key officers in the company was killed in a freak accident. It was at that moment that Joy knew what she had to do...she was going to join the family business.

Joy was the only daughter in a family of three boys. Although two of her brothers also worked in the business, her oldest brother at an independent subsidiary of RCCSC in Chicago, and the other as VP of Operations at the company's headquarters in Durham, there was no succession plan in place for any one of them to succeed her father. However, her father believed that it was Joy who should run the company. In 2001, he proceeded to name her President and CEO of the company. "It was both exciting and overwhelming at the same time, but I love a challenge," says Joy.

Because her father had been so intimately involved in the business, Joy was not prepared for what she encountered when she took over. Revenues were decreasing at an alarming rate. "My father was the 'chief' and the 'machine' behind sales, and because he was so personally involved in the business, when he got sick and could not be involved in the day-to-day operations, sales began to stagnate," says Joy. Revenues had plummeted to around $2 million. "Although my father was ill, it was the company that was in intensive care," recalls Joy. Not only did she have to quickly get up to speed on the business, clients, and so forth, her first order of business was developing a strategic plan to stop the downward spiral.

Her brother who ran the subsidiary in Chicago became her teacher on the ground. An expert salesman, she shadowed him to learn the business, how to make sales pitches, and so on. She was also flying back and forth between Durham and Atlanta, learning other aspects of the business from her father. They worked on strategic plans, and he would share stories of his contacts in each city, advising her whom she should reach out to. "It is funny how I would hear my father tell stories about the business, but they had no real relevance until I was faced with a similar situation," says Joy.

She made a plan to get on every major five- to ten-year project in markets across the country. She then went to every city where they had previously worked to introduce herself and to see what projects were coming up that they might be suited to pursue. She also sought to reduce the company's overhead and expenses. She made the decision to close expensive offices where they were not doing a great deal work, including Los Angeles and Miami.

The Mecca for African American Entrepreneurship

Prior to taking over the business, Joy had built a life in Atlanta and really did not want to move back to Durham to run the company. She was spending a lot of time flying back and forth between Durham and Atlanta to visit her mother and see her father for their study/ strategy sessions. However, she knew that she could not continue to function that way if she was going to really have an impact on the business. At the time, Atlanta was experiencing tremendous growth, becoming a mecca for African American entrepreneurship. Although the company conducted business all over the country, and could have moved anywhere, Joy figured this was a good time for the company to make a move, and she proposed that the company move its headquarters to Atlanta. Her father was not as enthusiastic about this idea, as the company had never been able to penetrate the market and successfully win projects like they had in other cities. However, her father trusted her judgment and told her that she could move the headquarters to Atlanta...if she landed a major contract, specifically at Hartsfield-Jackson Atlanta International Airport, one of the busiest airports in the country.

Like any new company into a market, it took a while for the locals to be open to an outsider and a woman coming in. She was even told she should pack it up and "go back to North Carolina, there was not enough work here to share." Joy knew there would be some pushback as a new firm coming into the area, but she was undeterred and took her time to learn the "players" and key decision-makers in Atlanta.

It took about a year, but she finally had the breakthrough she wanted. Not only did she win a contract but her company was named a joint venture partner with the Hartsfield-Jackson Construction Management Group. This joint venture provided construction services for major projects, including the fifth runway, at Hartsfield-Jackson Atlanta International Airport. The company has enjoyed this relationship for the past 13 years.

Breaking the Concrete Ceiling

Her strategic efforts have paid off. The company is going into its fifteenth year under her leadership, and today boasts revenues of $10 million and nearly 90 employees around the country. About a year ago, they reopened their offices in Los Angeles and Miami. "We are not the same size we were, but we are the right size for the market dynamics today," says Joy. "We are nimble and can respond to opportunities in most markets," she adds.

Another strategy that the company adopted is to become a local fixture in the markets where they have active projects. "We maintain a home as a residence, office space, et cetera in each major city where we have projects including Atlanta, Washington, DC, New York City, Los Angeles, Durham and Miami. This act goes a long way to show that we are not just there to get work but are contributing to the local economy," says Joy. "Growing up, I never knew why we had homes all over the country but now it makes sense. This is really a testament to my father's commitment to the communities in which we do business," she adds.

Her focus and versatility have also led to a variety of high-profile projects for RCCSC's resume, including contracts with Miami International Airport, the District of Columbia's Water and Sewer Authority, the Federal Highway Administration, and, of course, Hartsfield-Jackson, which she is most proud of.

Find a Mentor.

In addition to her father and her mother who always taught her to be confident but not arrogant, Joy credits Jerry Gray, who at the time was Deputy Chief of Staff for Governor Roy Barnes, with helping her to break through in Atlanta. "He helped me to make vital connections and key introductions throughout the City of Atlanta," says Joy. "He also helped me leverage the fact that we were an experienced firm with a solid history, which helped our story when trying to pursue work and develop partnerships," she adds.

Be Confident in Your Abilities.

Although she always considered herself capable and a quick learner, she had to work to prove herself to be a leader in a male-dominated field. Some of her colleagues have even congratulated her ability to sustain the company despite the barriers that exist in the industry.

"Men tell you exactly what they think, including where you stand. Working in this industry has been rewarding over the years and I've learned valuable lessons from my male counterparts." She goes on to say that, "Listening is truly an art and it allows you to become creative by stirring up new thoughts even if it's from a chauvinistic point of view."

Stay on Top of Your Game.

"When I think about how hard my father worked to gain respect in this industry, it reminds me that I must constantly stay focused on improving my skill set to build a stronger organization," she states. One of the ways that the company does this is by coaching and encouraging professional development for her staff. She even mentors students ranging from middle school to universities, particularly the female students, to encourage them to consider entrepreneurship or occupations in nontraditional fields. A frequent speaker on women's entrepreneurship and construction issues, Joy explains that this is not just key for her viability but is critical to helping women continue to gain the confidence to pursue business opportunities in this industry and become a stronger force.

While many firms shy away from complex projects, Joy actively seeks them out. "This is the only way that we can continue to expand our learning and offerings to our clients. In addition to our core competencies, this is how we can continue to create value," she adds.

Stay True to Who You Are

"I never lose sight that I am a woman operating in what has traditionally been a man's world. "Working in a male-dominated field has been both rewarding and challenging. Long hours, demanding schedules, sexist jokes and clear resentful intrusion are often the norm within the construction industry. My voice and opinions often fell on deaf ears, but over time I eventually gained the trust and respect of my male colleagues, by not wearing my emotions on my sleeve and proving to be competent and capable of operating in this arena," explains Joy. "I've learned that I don't have to work harder than my male colleagues, just smarter," she adds.

She has earned her place in this "man's world," and her colleagues have accepted her. She also found time to go back to school and earned her MBA in 2007.

50 Billion Dollar Boss Moves

When considering entrepreneurial opportunities in nontraditional fields, you should:

- Find a mentor;
- Be confident in your abilities;
- Stay on top of your game; and
- Stay true to who you are.

CHAPTER 13

Intrapreneurship: Adding Entrepreneurial Value and Innovation within a Corporation

Lisa Lambert, Vice President/Managing Director,
Software and Services and Diversity Equity Fund, Intel Capital

There has been a lot of talk lately about the success of women. Much of this discussion has been related to women in the corporate environment, the pay disparity experienced by women, and the lack of women on corporate boards and in senior level positions—more commonly referred to as the glass ceiling. While the economy is doing marginally better, women's pay is doing marginally worse.

For much of the past three decades, the wage gap between men and women began to shrink. But according to a new study from the Institute for Women's Policy Research, progress has slowed in recent years, and the wage gap has actually widened during the current recovery. In 2012, women working full time earned 80.9 percent of what men earned in terms of weekly pay—a drop from 82.2 percent in 2011, according to the IWPR study. In terms of annual earnings, women lagged men even further, making just 77 percent of what men earned, half a percentage point down from 2011. In dollar terms, that meant that women working full time earned an average of $691 a week in 2012, less than they had in 2011, while men earned $854 on average, which marked a small gain over their 2011 earnings. (The study did not evaluate men's and women's earnings in comparable jobs or life choices, and it excluded part-time jobs.) Compared to where they were earning decades ago, in many industries, women are closer to earning what men do. Progress had already been slowing for years, and this recent setback means that it may likely be even longer before women earn as much as men across all industries.

This stagnant growth is one of the reasons entrepreneurship has becoming increasingly attractive to women. However, not everyone has the luxury to strike out on her own. Thus, depending on the organization and its culture, intrapreneurship is increasingly becoming a viable option as it allows employees the opportunity to function like an entrepreneur, while working within a corporation. As more and more businesses are realizing the importance of nurturing and encouraging entrepreneurial thinking among their employees to help drive growth and innovation, intrapreneurship has become a way for women to exercise their entrepreneurial instincts without incurring the risks and uncertainty that full entrepreneurship requires.

Intrapreneurship has also thrived, as these employees are often highly valuable executives and team members who may perhaps never become a company founder, but are recognized for the value that they bring to the company. They have learned to apply the essential principles of entrepreneurship to the roles they play within an existing company and not to let bureaucratic barriers stop them from driving constructive change. Further, they have a strong understanding of the culture within which they are operating and have learned how to navigate around the roadblocks of corporate structure, tedious management, or the traditional corporate or government bureaucracy. Aditionally, they have convinced senior management that their new ideas have the potential to be both profitable and synergistic to the goals of the company, and are entrusted to bring their visions to life.

Lisa Lambert is Vice President and Managing Director of Software and Services and Diversity Equity Fund for Intel Capital. She shares her story of how her background in technology became the perfect fit in her role at Intel and how she created an opportunity to become the most accomplished and experienced African American woman in venture capital in the United States.

A Career Anomaly

Lisa's career in technology began after she obtained her BS in management information systems. She was trained in business information systems and compiled programming languages such as Cobol,

Pascal, Fortran, PL1, and in a number of application server development tools for Windows, MPE, and Unix operating system environments. Her first professional job was working as a software developer in the information technology (IT) department at Owens-Corning, where she supported IT operational functions and designed and debugged software in their manufacturing facilities and for their product groups. She had an aptitude for coding; however, she was ready to move her career to the next level. Yet she knew that in order to advance, she would need to get her MBA, so she quit her job and enrolled in Harvard University.

After earning her MBA from Harvard, she knew she wanted to join a technology company and live in California. She joined Intel Corporation in 1997 where she worked in technical marketing. She soon grew inquisitive about other opportunities at Intel as she did not feel she was using all of the skills she had acquired with her hard-earned MBA. She desired an opportunity to combine her technical background with her business acumen. Moving to Intel Capital seemed like an obvious fit.

"There are very few women in venture capital," says Lisa. "Black females? Almost none. Venture capital is an industry made up of private partnerships that recruit similar people from known networks, thereby resulting in an exclusive, rather than inclusive environment. In reality, it's a complete anomaly that I'm even in this game," she adds.

Knowing Your Worth

Over the next decade, Lisa was promoted every other year on her merits. She contributed to the company by making financially and strategically successful investments, and she was rewarded. By her tenth year, she aspired to be a corporate officer at the VP level. At Intel, this is a very big deal because the company placed significant value on the notion that great ideas can come from anywhere. They are cautious about titles that create a perception of hierarchy that might inhibit the free flow of innovation. As a result, very few VPs are named. It is a sophisticated process that involves more than a traditional performance review. Nominations are solicited through executive staff members, and a nominee's work is rigorously evaluated by the executive management committee, with veto rights given to Intel's CEO.

As Lisa considered applying, she saw strengths and weaknesses, but concluded that she had the data to support her case. The performance of her investment portfolio was solid, and her promotions spoke for themselves. Her staff and peer relationships were also a positive, though she needed to continue to network and reach out to other departments. Visibility is important, because the more people who can speak to a candidate's work, the more beneficial it is for the candidate.

It was an intimidating process with a very high failure rate, so it was critical for Lisa to throw herself into it and leave behind any fear and doubt. Like everything else that Lisa set out to accomplish, she developed a strategic approach to achieving this goal. She filled out the application and set meetings with several key decision-makers. By making her aspirations clear, she received support from several sponsors who had been advocating for her career development along the way as part of the Intel Network of Executive Women. "This network provided invaluable input and helped move my nomination forward," says Lisa. She continued her day-to-day work, determined to maintain a standard of excellence. Over the next several months, she anxiously awaited any news on the appointment. After a rigorous interview process (she interviewed with six people), she got the job.

When she finally received the news, she learned that not only had she earned the position but she had managed to secure it in her first year of application, which rarely happens. To her, this was like being inducted into the Hall of Fame. "It was a monumental achievement," recalls Lisa, "not so much about the appointment but by the fact that I had taken the risk and been recognized for my contribution and my potential."

By finding her niche within the organization, Lisa has been extremely successful. She achieved tremendous accomplishments and for the past ten years, her investments have realized a cumulative internal rate of return of 27 percent, with several of the companies she has invested in going public or being acquired. "My first investment to deliver an 800 percent return and my largest career investment of $218.5 million, were extraordinary experiences," says Lisa. "I enjoyed each of those moments and learned from all of them."

An Upward Calling

While Lisa has enjoyed a number of significant successes throughout her career, she considers the founding of her not-for-profit, Upward, as the most meaningful experience that she has had to date. The mission of Upward is to accelerate career advancement for senior professional women (director level and above). She began the organization in her home in 2013, when 90 women gathered for dinner and networking. The organization grew to over 1,500 members in 18 months. In 2014, she launched the first international chapter in Israel. Additional affiliates will be launched in London, England; Bangalore, India; Portland, Oregon; and Austin, Texas.

McKinsey and Company completed a study citing structural reasons why women do not advance professionally, including a lack of access to informal networks and a lack of mentors and sponsors. Lisa created Upward largely to address those problems in an attempt to change the demographics and culture in corporations globally, helping more women get a seat in both the boardroom and at the executive table. "It's difficult for me to imagine in the twenty-first century that women still only earn 77 cents for every dollar men earn for the same job," she says, "and that women only represent 12 percent of the Fortune 500 boards, 4 percent of the Fortune

500 CEO positions, and only 13 percent of the Fortune 500 executive office positions. This is despite the fact that women make up half of the world's population and, in America, women compose 51.5 percent of the professional workforce, earn the majority of college and advanced degrees, and head two-thirds of households. In the venture capital industry, the data is even more bleak, where only 4 percent of general partners are women and practically no minorities have any positions in the industry."

"My goal is to help change this with Upward, and in so doing, to help create wealth and prosperity for women that benefits society as a whole."

50 Billion Dollar Boss Moves

As more and more businesses are realizing the importance of nurturing and encouraging entrepreneurial thinking among their employees to help drive growth and innovation, to develop an "intrapreneurial" mind-set, you should:

- Know your worth;
- Make your aspirations clear;
- Maintain a standard of excellence;
- Develop a support system or join groups that can advocate for your success; and
- Find areas where you can create and add value.

CHAPTER 14

Make Being a Woman-Owned Business Work for You: Resources on Programs, Agencies, and Organizations That Support Women-Owned Businesses

No matter the industry or type of business you are looking to start, the decision to take the plunge to start a business can be a tough yet exhilarating decision. However, in today's economic climate, there is no reason to go at it alone or start from ground zero. There is an array of government agencies, private entities, and nonprofit organizations trying to bridge social and financial gaps with help directed specifically at minority women entrepreneurs. Finding that resource help often takes diligence and creativity—qualities that successful business owners tend to have. The services offered are varied, and are more than sufficient to help get you on your entrepreneurial way or accelerate the growth of your business.

Here are six agencies that can help you.

Small Business Administration

The US Small Business Administration (SBA) was created in 1953 as an independent agency of the federal government to aid, counsel, assist, and protect the interests of small business concerns, to preserve free competitive enterprise, and to maintain and strengthen the overall economy of our nation. The SBA recognizes that small business is critical to our economic recovery and strength, to building America's future, and to helping the United States compete in today's global marketplace. Although the SBA has grown and evolved in the years since it was established in 1953, the bottom-line mission remains the same: to help Americans start, build, and grow businesses. Through an extensive network of field offices and partnerships with public and private organizations, the SBA delivers its services to people throughout the United States, Puerto Rico, the US Virgin Islands, and Guam.

Service Corp of Retired Executives

Service Corp of Retired Executives (SCORE) is a nonprofit association dedicated to helping small businesses get off the ground, grow, and achieve their goals through education and mentorship. SCORE has played this role for nearly 50 years. Supported by the SBA, and through their network of over 11,000 volunteers, they deliver services at no charge or at very low cost.

Small Business Development Centers

Small Business Development Centers (SBDCs) provide a vast array of technical assistance to small businesses and aspiring entrepreneurs. By supporting business growth and sustainability, and enhancing the creation of new businesses entities, SBDCs foster local and regional economic development through job creation and retention. Through providing no-cost, extensive, one-on-one, long-term professional business advising, low-cost training, and other specialized services to clients, SBDCs remain one of the nation's largest small business assistance programs within the federal government. SBDCs are made up of a unique collaboration of SBA federal funds, state and local governments, and private sector resources.

National Women's Business Council

The National Women's Business Council (NWBC) is a nonpartisan federal advisory council created to serve as an independent source of advice and counsel to the president, Congress, and the US SBA on economic issues of importance to women business owners. The Council is the government's only independent voice for women entrepreneurs. Members are prominent women business owners and leaders of women's business organizations.

Minority Business Development Agency

Established in 1969, the Minority Business Development Agency (MBDA) is an agency of the US Department of Commerce that helps create and sustain US jobs by promoting the growth and global competitiveness of businesses owned and operated by minority entrepreneurs. The MBDA works throughout the nation to link minority-owned businesses with the capital, contracts, and markets they need to grow. They advocate and promote minority-owned business with elected officials, policy makers, and business leaders. Serving as subject matter experts and advocates for the minority business community, the MBDA conducts high-quality research and cultivates domestic and international relationships. Through a national network of more than 40 MBDA business centers and a wide range of domestic and international strategic partners, they provide technical assistance and access to capital, contracts, and new market opportunities to create new jobs. For example, over the four years from 2009 through 2012, the MBDA and its national network of business centers supported the creation and retention of more than 33,000 jobs and helped secure $14.6 billion in contracts and capital for its clients.

Women's Business Centers

A program of the SBA, Women's Business Centers (WBCs) represent a national network of nearly 100 educational centers designed to assist women in starting and growing small businesses.

Certifying Agencies

For years, certification has been the way to significantly help minority and women-owned businesses gain access to government "set aside contracts." Whether an individual is starting a business or her business is already established, a participant in certification programs can significantly benefit from these opportunities. Additionally, there are several government agencies at the local, state, and federal level that offer certification. Increasingly, certification has become a widely utilized tool by women-owned businesses to gain access to opportunities with corporate entities. Below are two of the most well-known agencies that offer certifications accepted by corporations.

National Minority Supplier Development Council

The National Minority Supplier Development Council (NMSDC) is the global leader in advancing business opportunities for its certified Asian, Black, Hispanic, and Native American business enterprises and connecting them to member corporations. NMSDC was chartered in 1972 to provide increased procurement and business opportunities for minority businesses of all sizes. The NMSDC Network includes 24 regional councils across the country. There are 1,700 corporate members throughout the network, including most of America's largest publicly owned, privately owned, and foreign-owned companies, as well as universities, hospitals, and other buying institutions. The regional councils certify and match more than 12,000 minority-owned businesses with member corporations that want to purchase their products, services, and solutions.

Women's Business Enterprise National Council

The Women's Business Enterprise National Council (WBENC), founded in 1997, is the largest third-party certifier of businesses owned, controlled, and operated by women in the United States. WBENC, a national 501(c)(3) nonprofit, partners with 14 regional partner organizations to provide its world-class standard of certification to women-owned businesses throughout the country. WBENC is also the nation's leading advocate of women-owned businesses as suppliers to America's corporations.

Supplier Diversity/MWBE (Minority/Women-Owned Business Enterprise) Programs—corporate, higher education, and so forth

Like the government, many corporations and higher education institutions have specific programs that target small, minority and women-owned entities in order to do business with them. These programs often conduct and participate in outreach conferences, vendor fairs, and matchmaking events in order to meet and engage with vendors. While the opportunities may vary, a potential participant should be sure to confirm whether any certifications are required for participation in their respective programs.

National Women's Business Advocacy Organizations

Below are a few national organizations that advocate and promote the success and sustainability of women-owned businesses:

- Association of Women's Business Centers
- National Association for Moms in Business
- National Association for Women Business Owners (NAWBO)
- Women Impacting Public Policy (WIPP)
- Women Presidents' Organization (WPO)
- GoldmanSachs 10,000 women
- Ernst & Young: Entrepreneurial Winning Women™
- SBA's Innovate: HER Business Challenge
- Upwardwomen.org

*All descriptions taken from agency/organization website

50 Billion Dollar Boss Moves

There are many programs designed specifically to help women-owned business succeed. To make being a woman-owned business work for you, you should:

- Seek out programs/organizations that specialize in women-owned businesses;
- Use collaboration to support and grow your business;
- Connect with networks with similar interests; and
- Cultivate a spirit of paying it forward.

Conclusion

While people of color are powering population growth in this country, African American women are helping drive business growth. Both of these realities make a clear case for breaking down barriers to entrepreneurship and supporting more equality in the workplace. Establishing more inclusive avenues for African American women to prosper as entrepreneurs will benefit not only women but also the economy as a whole. In fact, our economy cannot thrive if we do not work to bring more African American women out of poverty.

The inevitable demographic changes that will take place over the next few decades will provide the United States with the opportunity to empower African American women who are working to break through barriers. As a result, African American women will be afforded the opportunity to become a strong part of the US economic fabric as both entrepreneurs and innovators. Empowering African American women to capitalize on their own talents will help maximize their contributions to the economy at large by providing services, products, and jobs—all while contributing to their own families' economic stability. Closing racial and ethnic gaps will also increase economic growth, benefiting all Americans. In the recently published book *All-In Nation: An America that Works for All*, the Center for American Progress and PolicyLink present the gains that could be made through equity-driven growth. The authors calculated that if we had closed racial and ethnic gaps in income in 2011—by raising the wages of African Americans and Latinos to the levels of whites—average personal yearly income would have increased by 8.1 percent, and thirteen million people would have been lifted out of poverty.

While full access to funding streams, diverse industries, and networks is lacking for African American women, their entrepreneurial spirit and its impact on the economy are not. Women, and African American women in particular, face a wide array of obstacles and challenges, but their participation as business owners and employers is fundamental to the success of not only their own families and communities but also to the success of the US economy.

We hope that this book and these stories will inspire and inform you as you seek to take your business to new heights. Below is a summary of the tools and techniques that we have termed "50 Billion Dollar Boss Moves." These were shared in earlier chapters and should get you on the road to contributing to this dynamic revolution and becoming a 50 Billion Dollar Boss!

When turning your idea into a business, you should:
let inspiration find you;
find your mission;
have patience and perseverance; and
trust your instincts.

There are riches in the niches. To brand your passion and understand your unique value proposition, you should:
realize consultants do not always know what is best for your brand;
remember that every opportunity is not an opportunity for you;
seek out defining moments that make sense for the brand and your target; and
become the "champion" for your brand.

Attracting and building mentor relationships can be challenging. To attract the right mentors to help you and your business, you should:
think outside the "ideal" mentor box;
have several mentors;
realize every relationship has potential; and
create a reputation worthy of mentorship.

*To build strategic partnerships that add value and are mutually
beneficial, you should:*
choose partnerships that create value;
study the industry...yours and your potential partner's;
leverage partnerships to expand your reach and lower costs; and
use your network.

*Managing and cultivating relationships can be challenging.
To create a network to help grow your net worth,
you should:*
strive to build relationships that are more than just transactional;
stay engaged and in touch with your network;
understand that every kick can be a boost;
be consistent and deliberate when using social media;
be more interested than interesting; and
pay attention to industry trends, and know what is now but focus
on what is next.

*To determine the best solutions to fund your business and boost your
business development efforts, you should:*
create a plan outlining your long-term goals and objectives to
determine the right financing option;
focus on maximizing sales rather than incurring debt;
consider alternative funding options; and
consider collaboration to achieve your goals (a percentage of
something is better than 100% of nothing).

*Starting and running a business requires you to be healthy. To make
yourself a priority during this time, you should:*
develop a survivor mentality;
incorporate into your life activities that bring you joy and
fulfillment;
develop a supportive network; and
put *your* oxygen mask on first.

Change in business is inevitable. To keep things moving and to develop a resilient mind-set, you should:
focus time and energy on situations you can control;
not be afraid to try new things;
welcome adversity as a test for growth; and
stay committed to goals and objectives.

When trying to determine the best strategies to grow and scale your business, you should:
realize some open doors are a setup for failure;
ask for help;
step out of your comfort zone;
take advantage of unexpected events;
leverage your media exposure; and
not be afraid or intimidated to attract and pursue
"big investors."

Technology is presenting unprecedented opportunities for minorities and women. To take advantage of opportunities, you should:
not be afraid to consider opportunities in nontraditional fields;
consider the technological prospects in your industry;
realize that every meeting is a chance to build your network;
consider opportunities to develop new skills sets and experience
in technology; and
sometimes you have to go against the status quo.

When considering entrepreneurial opportunities in non-traditional fields, you should:
find a mentor;
be confident in your abilities;
stay on top of your game; and
stay true to who you are.

As more and more businesses are realizing the importance of nurturing and encouraging entrepreneurial thinking among their employees to help drive growth and innovation, to develop and "intrapreneurial" mind-set, you should:

know your worth;

make your aspirations clear;

maintain a standard of excellence;

develop a support system or join groups that can advocate for your success; and

find areas where you can create and add value.

There are many programs designed specifically to help women-owned businesses succeed. To make being a woman-owned business work for you, you should:

seek out programs/organizations that specialize in women-owned businesses;

use collaboration to support and grow your business;

connect with networks with similar interests; and

cultivate a spirit of paying it forward.

References

Reports

Ahmad, Farah, and Iverson, Sarah, *The State of Women of Color in the United States: Too Many Barriers Remain for This Growing and Increasingly Important Population*, www.AmericanProgress.org, October 24, 2013, accessed November 5, 2013.

American Express® OPEN, *Growing under the Radar: An Exploration of the Achievements of Million-Dollar Woman-Owned Firms*, January 2013, accessed November 12, 2013.

American Express® OPEN, *The 2014 State of Women-Owned Businesses Report*, 2013, http://www.womenable.com/userfiles/downloads/2013 State of Women-Owned Businesses Report FINAL.pdf, accessed March 15, 2014.

American Express® OPEN, *The 2013 State of Women-Owned Business Report*, accessed November 12, 2013.

American Express®OPEN, *Women and Minority Small Business Contractors: Divergent Paths to Equal Success*, 2012. A Research Summary for the American Express OPEN for Government Contracts: Victory in Procurement® (VIP), accessed November 12, 2013.

Center for Women's Business Research, *The Economic Impact of Women-Owned Businesses in the United States*, October 2009, Underwritten by Walmart and the National Women's Business Council and Center for Women's Business Research, https://www.nwbc.gov/sites/default/files/economicimpactstu.pdf, accessed October 2010.

Chang, Mariko, *Lifting as We Climb: Women of Color, Wealth, and America's Future*, March 2010, Full Paper (PDF), Executive Summary (PDF). Insight Center for Community Economic Development, www.racialwealthgap.org, accessed January, 2011.

Coleman, Susan, and Robb, Alicia, *Access to Capital by High-Growth Women-Owned Businesses*, SBAHQ-13-Q-0A63, 2013, National Women's Business Council, www.nwbc.org, accessed April 3, 2014.

Cox Business, *Majority of Women Entrepreneurs Optimistic about Business Success, Yet Still See Challenges*, 2013, Cox Business Snapshot of Women Entrepreneurs, http://www.coxblue.com/smbwomen/, accessed October 15, 2013.

Factors Influencing the Growth of Women-Owned Businesses: Risk Tolerance, Motivations, Expectations, Culture, 2013. Prepared for the National Women's Business Council, SBAHQ- 12-M-0206, www.nwbc.gov, accessed October 30, 2013.

Global Entrepreneurship Monitor 2012 Women's Report, 2011, www.gem-consortium.org, accessed February 25, 2013.

National Women's Business Council, *African American Women and Entrepreneurship Fact Sheet*, 2010, www.nwbr.org, accessed January 5, 2011.

National Women's Business Council, *African American Women-Owned Businesses*, 2012, http://www.nwbc.gov/facts/african-american-women-owned-businesses, accessed January 10, 2014.

National Women's Business Council, *Annual Report, 2012*, www.nwbc.org, accessed December 2, 2012.

National Women's Business Council, *Annual Report, 2013*, www.nwbc.org, accessed January 17, 2014.

Websites

Association of Women's Business Centers, www.awbc.biz.

Ernst & Young Entrepreneurial Winning Women™, www.ey.com.

Ewing Marion Kauffman Foundation, www.kauffman.com.

GoldmanSachs, 10,000 women, www.goldmansachs.com.

Minority Business Development Agency (MBDA), www.mbda.gov.

National Association for Moms in Business, www.momsinbusiness.org.

National Association for Women Business Owners (NAWBO), www.nawbo.org.

National Minority Supplier Development Council (NMSDC), www.nmsdc.org.

National Women's Business Council (NWBC), www.nwbc.org.

Progress 2050, Center for American Progress, www.americanprogress.org.
Service Corp of Retired Executives (SCORE), www.score.org.
Small Business Administration (SBA), www.sba.gov.
Small Business Development Center (SBDC), www.wbdc.org.
UPWARD (Uniting Professional Women Accelerating Relationships and Development), www.upwardwomen.org.
Women Impacting Public Policy (WIPP), www.wipp.org.
Women Presidents' Organization (WPO), www.womenpresidentsorg.com.
Women's Business Enterprise National Council (WBENC), www.wbenc.org.

Articles

Ahmad, Farah, "How Women of Color are Driving Entrepreneurship," Institute for Women's Policy Research, June 10, 2014, https://www.americanprogress.org/issues/race/report/2014/06/10/91241/how-women-of- color-are-driving-entrepreneurship/, accessed June 30, 2014.
Ahmad, Farah, "Idea of the Day: Why Are Many Women of Color Becoming Entrepreneurs?" June 11, 2014, https://www.americanprogress.org/issues/general/news/2014/06/11/91401/why-are- many-women-of-color-becoming-entrepreneurs/, accessed June 30, 2014.
Guynn, Jessica, "Google Backs 3-City Program for Black, Latino Techies," USA Today, March 16, 2015, www.USAToday.com, accessed March 31, 2015.
Penttila, Chris, "Minority Women Entrepreneurs: A Major Presence," July 5, 2007, Entrepreneur, www.entrepreneur.com, accessed May 2, 2013.
Simon, Ruth, and McGinty, Tom, "Loan Rebound Misses Black Businesses: Fewer SBA-Backed Loans Go To Black Borrowers," March 14, 2014, Wall Street Journal, www.wsj.com, accessed April 1, 2014.
Wirthman, Lisa, "Minority Women Entrepreneurs Are Leading the Way for Small Business Growth," July 15, 2013, Forbes, www.forbes.com, accessed October 22, 2013.

Books

Bundles, A'Lelia, On Her Own Ground: The Life and Times of Madam C. J. Walker, New York, NY: Scribner, 2001.

Fielden, Sandra L., and Davidson, Marilyn, *International Handbook of Women and Small Business Entrepreneurship*, Cheltenham, UK: Edward Elgar Publishing, 2005.

Hoskins, Michele, and Williams, Jean A., *Sweet Expectations: Michele Hoskins Recipe for Success*, Blue Ash, OH: Adams Media, 2004.

Lowry, Beverly, *Her Dream of Dreams: The Rise and Triumph of Madam C.J. Walker*, New York: Alfred A. Knopf, 2003.

Roche, Joyce, and Kopelman, Alexander, *The Empress Has No Clothes: Conquering Self Doubt to Embrace Success*, Oakland, CA: Berrett-Kohler Publishers, 2013.

Walker, Juliet, E. K., *The History of Black Business in America*, Chapel Hill, NC: University of North Carolina Press, 2009.

About the Authors

Kathey Porter

An expert on small business development, supplier diversity, and entrepreneurship, Kathey has been a Supplier Diversity Director and consultant for government, higher education, and corporate entities. She has been an adjunct business instructor at several colleges and universities, including Virginia Tech—Pamplin, College of Business, Savannah State University, Savannah College of Art & Design, Strayer University, Columbia College, and University of Phoenix.

Kathey was previously a marketing executive in the beauty industry, working on multicultural brands for companies including Carson Products, RevlonProfessional, and Colomer USA.

She has owned and operated several small businesses and recently founded BusinessFAB Enterprises, a multiplatform media initiative focused on the development of content, communications, customized networking events, and continuing education programs that connect women entrepreneurs to opportunities. Kathey received her MBA from Georgia Southern University and BBA from Savannah State University, and served as a Supply Specialist/Armor in the Georgia Army National Guard. Kathey has a daughter, Hollis, who is a sophomore at Virginia Tech, and a son, Mason.

Andrea Hoffman

Andrea Hoffman is a top-tier strategist, dealmaker, and business development veteran with over 23 years of experience. Her clients have included BMW, Credit Suisse, Hachette Filipacchi, Hermès, Jaguar, Carnegie Hall, Virginia Tech, Time Life, and Mercedes Benz USA. Since its inception in 2006, her consultancy, Culture Shift Labs has helped companies understand, access and engage untapped consumer markets and overlooked business opportunities. It has also paved the way for countless deals and growth opportunities for and with the "diverse elite," a 840-billion-dollar market. Andrea is the co-author of *Black is the New Green: Marketing to Affluent African Americans* and the author of *Re-Fraggle: How and Why Diverse Teams Achieve Breakthrough Innovation.*

Index